The Hong Kong Economic Policy Studies Series

HONG KONG AND SOUTH CHINA:

THE ECONOMIC SYNERGY

T0294465

HONG KONG
AND
SOUTH CHINA:
THE
ECONOMIC SYNERGY

Yun-Wing Sung

Published for
The Hong Kong Centre for Economic Research
The Better Hong Kong Foundation
The Hong Kong Economic Policy Studies Forum
by

City University of Hong Kong Press

First published 1998
Printed in Hong Kong

ISBN 962-937-015-8

Published by
City University of Hong Kong Press
City University of Hong Kong
Tat Chee Avenue, Kowloon, Hong Kong

Internet: http://www.cityu.edu.hk/upress/
E-mail: upress@cityu.edu.hk

The free-style calligraphy on the cover, *nan*, means "South" in Chinese.

Contents

Detailed Chapter Contents

Foreword

The key to the economic success of Hong Kong has been a business and policy environment which is simple, predictable and transparent. Experience shows that prosperity results from policies that protect private property rights, maintain open and competitive markets, and limit the role of the government.

The rapid structural change of Hong Kong's economy in recent years has generated considerable debate over the proper role of economic policy in the future. The restoration of sovereignty over Hong Kong from Britain to China has further complicated the debate. Anxiety persists as to whether the pre-1997 business and policy environment of Hong Kong will continue.

During this period of economic and political transition in Hong Kong, various interested parties will be re-assessing Hong Kong's existing economic policies. Inevitably, they will advocate an agenda aimed at altering the present policy making framework to reshape the future course of public policy.

For this reason, it is of paramount importance for those familiar with economic affairs to reiterate the reasons behind the success of the economic system in the past, to identify what the challenges are for the future, to analyze and understand the economy sector by sector, and to develop appropriate policy solutions to achieve continued prosperity.

In a conversation with my colleague Y. F. Luk, we came upon the idea of inviting economists from universities in Hong Kong to take up the challenge of examining systematically the economic policy issues of Hong Kong. An expanding group of economists (The Hong Kong Economic Policy Studies Forum) met several times to give form and shape to our initial ideas. The Hong Kong Economic Policy Studies Project was then launched in 1996 with some 30 economists from the universities in Hong Kong and a few from overseas. This is the first time in Hong Kong history that a concerted public effort has been undertaken by academic economists in the territory. It represents a joint expression of our collective concerns, our hopes for a better Hong Kong, and our faith in the economic future.

The Hong Kong Centre for Economic Research is privileged to be co-ordinating this Project. We are particularly grateful to The Better Hong Kong Foundation whose support and assistance has made it possible for us to conduct the present study, the results of which are published in this monograph. The unfailing support of many distinguished citizens in our endeavour and their words of encouragement are especially gratifying. We also thank the directors and editors of the City University of Hong Kong Press and The Commercial Press (H.K.) Ltd. for their enthusiasm and dedication which extends far beyond the call of duty.

Yue-Chim Richard Wong
Director
The Hong Kong Centre
for Economic Research

Foreword by the Series Editor

Since the last century, the main economic ties of Hong Kong with the outside world have been those with South China. Most of such ties were severed in the early 1950s however when the United Nations imposed a trade embargo on China following the outbreak of the Korea War. With the Chinese economy moved rapidly towards central planning, Hong Kong then had to turn to develop and expand economic relations with the West in the ensuing decades.

China embarked on economic reform and opened up its economy in the late 1970s. Since then, Hong Kong has, in an economic sense, recaptured the hinterland in South China, especially Guangdong Province. Integration between the economies of Hong Kong and Mainland China forged ahead.

The economic integration between Hong Kong and South China is not taking place at all fronts. Most prominently, there is no integration in the labour market, monetary arrangements and fiscal concerns. Labour mobility from the Mainland to Hong Kong is highly restricted. The two economies continue to have different currencies and monetary systems, and their government budgets are independent of each other. Nevertheless, the integration has proceeded with such scope and pace that the whole South China, including Hong Kong, has greatly transformed since the mid-1980s. Today, the South China region covering Hong Kong, Guangdong, Fujian and Taiwan has become a major trading area with vibrant cross-border direct investments.

How did economic interactions in South China take place? What is the situation of trade and investment flows within the region? How important is the region relative to other major economic blocs in the world? From Hong Kong's perspective, what are the benefits and costs of being the core economy in this regional integration? What are the future prospects of the whole area? What are the relevant policy considerations?

This book deals with all these issues. Although it focuses on Hong Kong and Guangdong, the books pays due coverage to Taiwan, Fujian, and Shanghai. It traces the changes in government policies and institutions in the respective economies. Using consistent indicators, it pulls together official figures and surveys and presents a clear picture of economic activities, especially trade and direct investment, that have been going on in the region.

Recent commentators have espoused the idea of promoting the so-called "Chinese Economic Area". While economic restructuring in Hong Kong and South China has been a result of China's opening up, concrete policies to further integration in any specific manner may or may not be warranted. This book analyzes some policy proposals such as the formation of a trading bloc, the establishment of "bonded areas", and the co-ordination of infrastructure development between Hong Kong and South China.

The author of this book, Professor Yun Wing Sung, is a long-time researcher in the economic synergy between the Chinese Mainland and Hong Kong. He has written extensively on the subject and this book represents his most updated views and findings. So it is a valuable reference for discussing the future of the Hong Kong economy in the regional context.

Y. F. Luk
School of Economics and Finance
The University of Hong Kong

Preface

This project is supported by the Better Hong Kong Foundation and also by a grant from the Research Grants Council of Hong Kong (CUHK 165/94H). I would like to thank Y. F. Luk, the Series Editor, and an anonymous referee for helpful comments. The Census and Statistics Department of the Hong Kong Government has kindly provided unpublished data for this book. My thanks also go to Dr. Chan Chi Shing and Mr. Banny Lam for their able research assistance.

Yun-Wing Sung
Department of Economics
The Chinese University of
Hong Kong

October 1998

List of Illustrations

Acronyms and Abbreviations

Acronyms	Names in Full	Appear First on Page
APEC	Asian-Pacific Economic Community	164
ASEAN	Association of South-East Asian Nations	39
BOC	Bank of China	100
CEA	Chinese Economic Area	1
c. i. f.	Cost, Insurance and Freight	19
CITIC	China International Trust and Investment Company	103
EC	European Community	49
EEC	European Economic Community	49
EU	European Union	49
FDI	Foreign Direct Investment	6
f. o. b.	Free on Board	19
FTA	Free Trade Areas	48
GATT	General Agreement on Tariff and Trade	48
GDP	Gross Domestic Product	3
HIT	Hong Kong International Terminals Limited	149
HKSAR	Hong Kong Special Administrative Region	3
MFA	Multi-fibre Arrangement	141
MFN	Most Favoured Nations	48
MOFERT	Ministry of Foreign Economic Relations and Trade	14
MOFTEC	Ministry of Foreign Trade and Economic Cooperation	166
NCNA	New China News Agency	107
PLA	People's Liberation Army	108
P&O	Peninsular & Oriental Stream Navigation Co.	149
SEZ	Special Economic Zone (SEZ)	33
"the trio"	Mainland China, Hong Kong SAR, Taiwan	12
WTO	World Trade Organization	48

Hong Kong and South China:
The Economic Synergy

Map
The South China Region in the China Circle

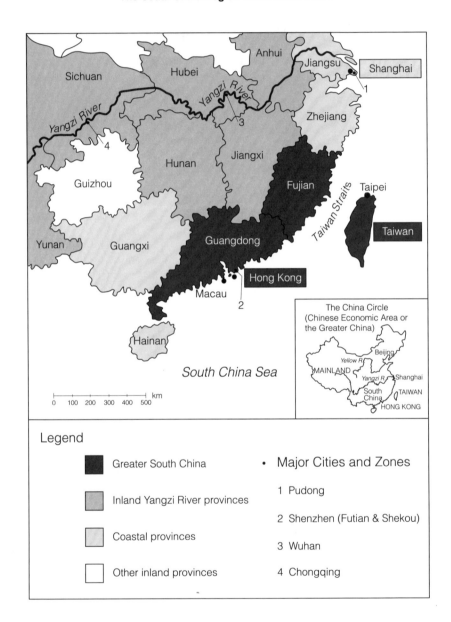

Legend

■ Greater South China

▨ Inland Yangzi River provinces

▨ Coastal provinces

☐ Other inland provinces

• Major Cities and Zones

1 Pudong

2 Shenzhen (Futian & Shekou)

3 Wuhan

4 Chongqing

CHAPTER 1

Introduction

Three Layers of the China Circle

Since the inauguration of China's open-door policy in 1979, extremely intense trade and investment flows have developed between Hong Kong and the Mainland and between Taiwan and the Mainland. The China Circle, which includes Hong Kong, Macau, Taiwan, and the Mainland, has become a dynamic region that has a substantial impact on world trade and investment.

In terms of the degree of economic integration, there are three concentric layers of the China Circle (see the map on the opposite page). The Hong Kong–Guangdong economic nexus or Greater Hong Kong is the core; Greater South China covering Hong Kong, Guangdong, Fujian, and Taiwan is the inner layer, and Greater China or the Chinese Economic Area (CEA) covering Hong Kong, Macau, Taiwan, and the Mainland is the outer layer. Hong Kong is the pivot for the integration of the China Circle.

The impetus for the integration of the CEA came about primarily as a result of the opening and reform of China and also in part as a result of the economic liberalization of Taiwan. Despite economic liberalization, there are still many barriers to economic integration of the CEA. Foremost among these are the remnants of central economic planning in China and Taiwan's ban on direct business links with the Mainland. And there is no institutional framework co-ordinating the economic integration of the CEA. However, geographic and cultural proximity and the huge gains from economic complementarity are overcoming the many barriers to economic interaction. Private initiative and market forces have led to intense trade and investment flows within the CEA despite the lack of an institutional framework.

This book will concentrate on the Hong Kong–Guangdong nexus, which is the core of the China Circle. It will also cover Greater South China and the CEA, as the discussion of these regions provides the overall context for the development of Greater Hong Kong. Moreover, statistics on international trade are much more detailed on the level of the Mainland as a whole than on the provincial level, and it is much easier to analyze Hong Kong's trade with China than Hong Kong's trade with Guangdong or Fujian.

It should be noted that South China is broader in scope than Guangdong is. It can be argued that South China includes the whole region south of the Yangzi (see map). However, for our purpose, this definition of South China is too broad to be useful, as Hong Kong's links with the inland provinces south of the Yangzi (e.g., Sichuan, Hunan, and Jiangsi) are not particularly intense. It should be also noted that, in China's Ninth Five-Year Plan, China is divided into seven regions, and the southeastern region covers Guangdong and Fujian. The southeastern region forms the mainland part of Greater South China. This book will concentrate on the southeastern seaboard (including Taiwan) where the links with Hong Kong are intense. Shanghai is also covered where appropriate, as its link with Hong Kong is significant. Moreover, Shanghai is also important, as the focus of China's development shifted from Guangdong to Shanghai with the opening of Pudong in 1990.

The Reintegration of Greater South China

Hong Kong lost its hinterland (Guangdong and South China) in the Cold War Era and regained it in 1979 with the opening of China. Greater South China, which was divided by the Cold War, started to reintegrate in 1979. In Hong Kong's economic history, each new phase of economic development was caused by a fundamental shift in Hong Kong's relationship with the hinterland. There have been three fundamental shifts since the post-war era. The first shift occurred in 1950 with the outbreak of the Korean War and the beginning of the Cold War in East Asia. During this time, in addition to losing its hinterland, Hong Kong also lost its entrepôt trade. It survived by virtue of an economic miracle of export-oriented industrialization, and the United States was the number one market for Hong Kong manufactured goods. From the 1950s to the 1970s Hong Kong grew as part of *pax Americana* instead of as part of China.

The second shift occurred in 1979 with the opening of China, when Hong Kong partially regained its hinterland. Reintegration was incomplete, as mainland labour could not come to Hong Kong, while Hong Kong capital was quite free to move into the Mainland, especially to invest in manufacturing. Since then, Hong Kong's labour-intensive industries have largely relocated to Guangdong, and Hong Kong's investment in the Mainland has transformed the economies of both the Mainland and Hong Kong. However, the economic integration achieved was quite shallow, as it was largely restricted to the integration of the manufacturing sector. Integration of services has been slow, partly because of China's restrictions on external investment in services, and partly because of Hong Kong's barriers to migration.

The third shift occurred in July 1997 with the establishment of the Hong Kong Special Administrative Region (HKSAR) of China. This shift will likely herald the deep reintegration of Hong Kong with its hinterland. Today, Hong Kong is much more of a service hub than a manufacturing centre where services and manufacturing, respectively, accounted for 84% and 7% of the Gross Domestic Product (GDP) in 1996. It should gain much more from the integration of services than from the integration of manufacturing.

The Hinterland — Advantages and Disadvantages

The hinterland supplies food, labour, markets, and business opportunities to the metropolis. The hinterland may also be a reservoir of backwardness, poverty, population pressure, and illiteracy. Before 1997 Hong Kong was able to maintain strict barriers against mainland migrants. It has been able to avoid the massive immigration and unemployment typical in many Third World cities. In its relations with the hinterland, Hong Kong has been able to make use of most of the advantages and avoid the greater part of the disadvantages. However, the strict barriers against mainland migrants to Hong Kong may erode now that 1997 has come and gone, and it is likely that Hong Kong has to take the bad along with the good.

The First Shift: Loss of the Hinterland and Export-Oriented Industrialization

The peculiarity of Hong Kong's export-oriented industrialization was that it had been partially cut off from its hinterland soon after 1950. Hong Kong benefited from the low-cost foodstuffs and potable water China supplied it. However, the Hong Kong government sealed the border against migration in 1949. Many refugees did make their way to Hong Kong, nevertheless. China did not accept investment from Hong Kong or anywhere else, and it imported very little from Hong Kong in the 1950s.

As Hong Kong's economic miracle is founded on the export of labour-intensive manufactured goods, it was not in Hong Kong's interest to cut off the flow of refugees completely. The government regulated illegal migration through the so-called "touch base" policy: Refugees who evaded capture and managed to establish contact with a family member or friend were defined as having touched base and were allowed to stay, but those who were caught before doing so were repatriated to China. The policy could be used to regulate Hong Kong's labour market, as the government could passively permit more illegal migrants to enter by relaxing the efforts of interdiction during periods of labour shortage. Though Hong Kong's export-led economic miracle caused employment to rise rapidly beginning in the 1950s, waves of illegal migrants from China had replenished the labour supply, and the labour market had not been too tight.

Because of the peculiar way in which Hong Kong was estranged from its hinterland, it was able to enjoy the advantages of the hinterland without suffering its disadvantages. Hong Kong continued to enjoy a steady supply of food from the hinterland. It also obtained

enough refugee labour for its labour-intensive industries. Compared with regular migrants from the hinterland, refugees adapted
to industrial discipline much faster because their backs were to the
wall and they could not go home. They made much better industrial
workers. Hong Kong was spared the many problems of rural migration and return migration, namely unemployment, high labour
turnover, poor sanitation, and contagious diseases.

The Second Shift: China's Opening and Shallow Reintegration

The loosening of social controls in China after Mao's death led to
an influx of over 0.5 million legal and illegal immigrants into Hong
Kong from 1976 to 1980. In 1980 alone 200,000 illegal immigrants
entered Hong Kong. As a result of the rapid rise in per capita income
in Hong Kong and the improved social services and social welfare,
unskilled immigrants were regarded as a liability rather than an
asset. Moreover, unlike the refugees of the 1950s who fled from
political upheaval, illegal immigrants of the late 1970s were primarily looking for better economic opportunities. They enjoyed little
public sympathy.

The Hong Kong government terminated the "touch base"
policy in late 1980 and instituted a system of computerized identity
cards that residents must carry in public. Illegal immigrants who are
caught are promptly repatriated to China.

According to the treaties that ceded Hong Kong to Britain,
Chinese had the right to enter Hong Kong, and the Hong Kong
government could not impose an immigration quota. However, to
demonstrate its goodwill during the Sino-British negotiations in the
early 1980s over the future of Hong Kong, China agreed to an exit
quota of legal migrants of seventy-five per day.

As a result of the termination of the "touch base" policy, the
labour market in Hong Kong became very tight starting in 1986.
From 1987 to 1994 the annual unemployment rate in Hong Kong
never rose above 2%. With the rapid rise in wages that occurred in
Hong Kong in the late 1980s, the human capital that Hong Kong
manufacturers had accumulated in the production and export of
labour-intensive products would have been obsolete if Hong Kong

firms had not relocated to economies that still had abundant labour. However, most manufacturing firms in Hong Kong were small and ill-equipped to operate across geographic and cultural barriers. China had the advantage of geographic and cultural proximity, and the opening of China presented a golden opportunity to Hong Kong manufacturing firms, which relocated to the Mainland in droves.

The main destination of Hong Kong manufacturing firms has been Guangdong Province. At the end of 1996, Guangdong accounted for around 40% of Hong Kong's cumulative FDI (Foreign Direct Investment) in China and around 30% of all cumulative FDI in China.

Blessings of Reintegration

The successful reintegration of Hong Kong with its hinterland brought prosperity to both Hong Kong and China, and this prosperity quickly overshadowed the gloom that followed the Tiananmen incident of 1989. The net emigration of permanent Hong Kong residents reached a peak of 48,100 in 1990 but declined to 38,900 and 24,100, respectively, in 1991 and 1992.

The successful economic development in Guangdong has strengthened the reforms in China. Deng Xiaoping toured Guangdong early in 1992 and designated Guangdong as the "dragon head" of China's economic reforms. Investors in Hong Kong responded immediately to the change. Hong Kong's contracted FDI in China jumped from US$7 billion in 1991 to US$40 billion in 1992 and again to US$74 billion in 1993. Hong Kong's net emigration of permanent Hong Kong residents also turned abruptly into a net immigration of 1,100 in 1993, increasing rapidly to a net immigration of 63,900 in 1996 and over 120,000 in 1997. The 1996 population of Hong Kong was 407,000 above that projected by the Hong Kong government in 1992, largely because of the sudden influx of returning migrants.

Hong Kong's investment in Guangdong has transformed both economies. Hong Kong manufacturing firms reportedly employed up to 6 million workers in Guangdong, while the manufacturing labour force in Hong Kong fell from a record of 905,000 in 1984 to 288,887 by the end of 1997. By moving the labour-intensive processes to Guangdong, Hong Kong has been able to concentrate on more skill-intensive processes such as product design, sourcing, production management, quality control, and marketing. Hong Kong manufacturing has thus achieved a very high rate of labour productivity growth. The expansion of exports from processing operations in Guangdong also increased the demand for Hong Kong's service industries, including entrepôt trade, shipping, insurance, business services, and financial services. Both the Hong Kong manufacturing sector and the Hong Kong economy have become increasingly service oriented. In short, Hong Kong has become the economic capital of an industrialized Guangdong.

The Third Shift: Deep Integration after Restoration of Hong Kong to China?

The adjustment to Hong Kong's reversion to Chinese rule in 1997 occurred well before 1997 because it was known that the handover would take place fourteen years in advance, with the signing of the Sino-British Declaration in 1984. For instance, mainland investors started stepping up their investment in Hong Kong in 1984 because they considered Hong Kong their future turf. Hong Kong capitalists could acquire goodwill by investing in China or by helping Chinese companies invest in Hong Kong.

Many Hong Kong firms have acquired useful China connections through such investments, and they are well positioned to take advantage of the liberalization of services in China. For instance, in June 1997, just before the reversion of Hong Kong to China, Cable and Wireless sold 5.5% of the shares of Hong Kong Telecommunications (one of the largest firms in Hong Kong in terms of employment and stock market capitalization) to China's Ministry of Post and Telecommunications. Mainland partners will eventually have controlling interest of Hong Kong Telecommunications, which is well positioned to take advantage of the vast opportunities in China's telecommunications market.

After Deng Xiaoping's 1992 southern tour, China started to lift some of the restrictions on foreign investment in the services sectors, though the liberalization has been slow. As services are performed on people, cultural and geographic proximity is even more important than it is for goods production. Given Hong Kong's comparative advantage in services, the liberalization of services in China should bring tremendous benefits to Hong Kong.

Hong Kong's restoration to China will facilitate the integration process. With the Sino-British disputes out of the way, Hong Kong and the Mainland will find it easier to co-ordinate infrastructure developments and economic policies. Policy co-ordination is especially important in the integration of services, because services such as banking, insurance, and telecommunications are often highly regulated.

Taking the Good with the Bad

Although the advantages of reintegration are many, it is also likely to effect the erosion of Hong Kong's strict controls against migration from the Mainland. Hong Kong will face the pressures of population growth and unemployment.

Hong Kong residents have large numbers of family members in China. Since the establishment of China's exit quota in 1982, spouses of Hong Kong residents have often had to wait ten years or more to migrate to Hong Kong. To alleviate the pressure, China raised the exit quota with the agreement of the Hong Kong government from 75 per day to 105 per day in 1993 and then to 150 per day in 1995.

The rate of population growth in Hong Kong is expected to be high in the long run, largely because of immigration from the Mainland. According to the 1997 population projection of the Hong Kong government, population will grow at the average annual rate of 1.4% in the near future, rising from 6.3 million in mid-1966 to 7.8 million in 2011. This is 1.3 million more than the previous projection made in 1992.

The government projection is most likely an underestimate because it puts the number of immigrants from China at the current exit quota imposed by China (150 per day). The pressure for relaxing the quota will increase, as many Hong Kong residents have family members in the Mainland. According to a government survey in 1992, there were 405,400 direct relatives (95,200 spouses and 310,200 children) of Hong Kong residents living in China in 1991 (Census and Statistics Department, Hong Kong, 1993: pp. 115–126). From 1991 to 1996, 214,000 of these entered Hong Kong, but the stock in China had risen to 432,600 (112,000 spouses and 320,600 children) by the end of 1995, as the number of Hong Kong–Mainland marriages increased (Census and Statistics Department, Hong Kong, 1997a, pp. 1–5).

According to the Basic Law, the children of Hong Kong residents born outside Hong Kong are also Hong Kong residents, and they have a constitutional right to stay in Hong Kong. Of the over 320,000 children of Hong Kong residents in the Mainland, an estimated 66,000 (July 1997 figure) were born after their parents had already become permanent residents of Hong Kong, and they have the right to enter Hong Kong. The rest may also have the same right, depending on the interpretation of the Basic Law. The HKSAR Government has passed a law to delay their immediate entry, and the law is being contested in court. Whatever the outcome, the number of immigrants from China will likely increase substantially. The present immigration controls, though supported by Beijing, are quite discriminatory against mainlanders. In contrast to the problems faced by spouses and children of Hong Kong residents living in China, those in other places can enter Hong Kong with little difficulty, because they do not face an exit quota.

While immigration is the focus of another book in the Hong Kong Economic Policy Studies Series and will not be dealt with in any depth here, it must be stressed that the immigration policy is one of the most important instruments at the disposal of the Hong Kong government. Most people agree that Hong Kong should attract more skilled migrants from China; many commentators wish to maintain the present stringent controls on family reunion. However, economic integration naturally implies more person-to-person contacts and cross-border marriages. Hong Kong cannot reap the benefits of reintegration and avoid its pitfalls forever. The present stringent controls disrupt family life and impose huge social and economic costs on a very large number of people. Such controls are inhumane, unwise, and indefensible. It would be preferable to reduce the economic incentive of migration and let individuals make the decision to locate their families in Hong Kong or the Mainland. For instance, Hong Kong could impose length-of-residency requirements on social services and social welfare.

As long as "one country, two systems" exists, migration from the Mainland to Hong Kong will not be entirely free. However, the pool of potential migrants is so large that Hong Kong will face considerable population pressure if there is even a slight erosion of migration barriers. The present quota of 150 per day amounts to 54,760 immigrants per year, and this alone implies a 1997 population growth of 0.85%, which exceeds the rate of natural growth. It is clear that Hong Kong has to be prepared for the pressures of population growth, unemployment, and income maldistribution.

The ultimate solution for population pressure in Hong Kong may lie in closer ties with the Mainland. Presently, there are some Hong Kong residents who live in the Mainland and commute to work in Hong Kong. However, commuting is inconvenient due to congested border crossings. Expanding the capacity of border crossings will facilitate commuting. Hong Kong can also encourage retired people to move to the Mainland by building housing estates in Shenzhen designed for retirees.

Taiwan and the Reintegration of Greater South China

Taiwan's separation from the Mainland in the Cold War was much more drastic than the separation of the Mainland from Hong Kong. In Taiwan's case, virtually all links with the Mainland — including commodity trade, mail, transport, and telecommunications — were severed in 1950. Partial reintegration occurred in the 1980s,

Table 1.1

Basic Indicators of Greater China, 1997

Indicators	Hong Kong	Taiwan	Macau	China	Guangdong	Fujian	Shanghai
Area (sq. km.)	1,068	36,006	19	960,000	177,901	121,400	6,341
Population (million)	6.50	21.68	0.42	1,236	70.51	32.82	14.57
GDP (US$ billion)	171.4	283.7	7.3	902.1	88.2	36.2	40.5
Per capita GDP (US$)	26,362	13,157	17,372	730	1,255	1,107	3,105
1997 GDP growth rate (%)	5.2	6.6	−0.12	8.8	10.6	14.3	12.7
Exports (US$ billion)	188.1[a] 27.3[b]	122.1	2.1	182.7	75.9	11.0	14.8

Sources: Data for China, Guangdong and Fujian come from the respective *Statistical Yearbooks of China*. Data for Hong Kong come from the *Hong Kong Monthly Digest of Statistics*, Census and Statistics Department, Hong Kong. Data for Taiwan are taken from the *Monthly Bulletin of Statistics of the Republic of China*, Directorate General of Budget, Accounting and Statistics, Executive Yuan, Republic of China. Data for Macau are taken from the Web.

Note: (a) Total exports (including re-export).
(b) Domestic exports (exports of Hong Kong goods).

though the process was slow because of the political differences between the Mainland and Taiwan.

The heart of this book is the reintegration of Hong Kong with its hinterland that has been taking place since 1979. The partial reintegration of Taiwan and Greater South China will also be covered, as Taiwan is part of the "natural economic territory" of the southern region of China.[1]

Basic Economic Indicators

Table 1.1 shows the 1996 basic economic indicators of the China Circle, including the Mainland, Hong Kong, Macau, Taiwan, Guangdong, Fujian, and Shanghai. The GDP (Gross Domestic Product) of Taiwan was 1.7 times that of Hong Kong. Comparing the GDP of Hong Kong and Taiwan to that of China or its provinces is not meaningful, because the GDP of China is biased downwards as a result of price differences. Comparison of export values may be more meaningful.

China's 1997 exports of US$183 billion surpassed Taiwan's exports of US$122 billion and also vastly surpassed Hong Kong's domestic exports (i.e., exports made domestically in Hong Kong) of US$27 billion. Hong Kong's total exports (i.e., including re-exports) of US$188 billion still exceeded China's exports by a large margin, but only because Hong Kong was re-exporting Chinese products to third countries and third-country products to China. In other words, Hong Kong is China's gateway to the world in commodity trade.

Guangdong's 1997 exports of US$76 billion vastly exceeded Hong Kong's domestic exports of US$27 billion and also surpassed Thailand exports of US$57 billion. It should be noted that Fujian was a distant second to Guangdong in terms of economic strength. Fujian's 1997 exports and GDP were only 14% and 41% of Guangdong's, respectively. A majority of Taiwanese originate from Fujian, and Taiwan accounted for the bulk of the FDI in Fujian. However, the prime destination of Taiwanese investment in China is still Guangdong, because of Guangdong's economic dynamism.

Despite its recent rapid growth, Shanghai is much less export-oriented than Guangdong is. In 1997 Shanghai's GDP was 46% of Guangdong's, but the value of Shanghai's exports was only 19% of that of Guangdong's. This is because of the legacy of China's import-substitution strategy instigated in the pre-reform era. Under protection, Shanghai built up a vast industrial complex composed of state-owned enterprises, and the protected industries were often inefficient. The inefficiencies of import substitution and state ownership have handicapped the development of Shanghai up to the present.

Macau's economy is much smaller than that of Hong Kong and can be regarded as an appendage of the Hong Kong economy. This book will concentrate on the economic interdependence among China, Hong Kong and Taiwan, or the "trio", and there will be no separate treatment of Macau.

The Emergence of Guangdong

Due to its connections with Hong Kong, Guangdong has risen rapidly from a comparatively backward province to the leading province in China in the reform era. In the eighteen years from 1978 to 1996, China has been the fastest-growing economy in the world, growing at the average annual rate of 9.9%. In the same period, Guangdong grew at the average annual rate of 14%, more than four percentage points above the national average. Guangdong, which ranked seventh in its GDP among the provinces in 1978, rose to the top in 1989.

Table 1.2 (on next page) compares the shares of Guangdong and Shanghai in China's GDP, industrial output, value added of the tertiary sector, and exports. In 1978 Shanghai's share of China's GDP, industrial output, and exports was 7.5%, 12.1%, and 29.7%, respectively — the highest among the provinces. However, Guangdong grew much faster than Shanghai did and surpassed Shanghai in GDP in 1983, in exports in 1986, and in industrial output in 1989. Guangdong has been China's number one province in inward foreign investment since 1979, in exports since 1986, in GDP since 1989, and in industrial output since 1995.

The opening of Pudong in 1990 failed to shrink the gap between Guangdong and Shanghai. From 1990 to 1997 Shanghai's share of China's GDP rose marginally from 4.1% to 4.5%. Meanwhile, Guangdong's share rose markedly from 7.9% to 9.8%. From 1990 to 1997 Shanghai's share of China's industrial output dropped markedly, from 6.9% to 5.0%, but Guangdong's share rose from 8% to 9.7%. Shanghai also performed poorly in terms of exports. Its share of national exports dropped from 10.2% to 8.1%, while Guangdong's share rose from 35.8% to 41.6%. Shanghai only performed well in services. Its share of the value added of China's tertiary sector rose from 4.2% to 6.4%. Guangdong's share also rose from 8.6% to 11%, and the gap in service output between

Table 1.2

**Share of Shanghai and of Guangdong in China's GDP,
Industrial Output, and Exports, 1978–97
(%)**

	Share of Shanghai in China's				Share of Guangdong in China's			
	GDP	Industrial Output	Value Added (Tertiary Sector)	Exports	GDP	Industrial Output	Value Added (Tertiary Sector)	Exports
1978	7.5	12.1	5.9	29.7	5.1	4.7	5.1	14.2
1979	6.7	11.9	6.2	26.9	5.0	4.6	5.8	12.5
1980	6.9	11.6	6.8	23.3	5.4	4.3	6.4	12.0
1981	6.7	11.5	6.7	18.2	5.9	5.0	6.8	11.4
1982	6.4	10.9	6.5	16.5	6.3	5.1	7.0	10.3
1983	6.0	10.3	6.3	16.4	6.1	5.1	6.5	10.7
1984	5.4	9.6	5.6	14.7	6.1	5.3	6.4	10.2
1985	5.2	8.9	4.8	13.0	6.2	5.5	6.1	11.4
1986	4.8	8.5	4.6	13.3	6.3	5.6	6.8	**15.7**
1987	4.6	7.8	4.6	12.0	6.8	6.4	7.3	25.7
1988	4.3	7.2	4.2	11.3	7.4	7.2	7.7	31.2
1989	4.1	6.9	3.7	11.6	7.8	7.5	8.0	34.5
1990	4.1	6.9	4.2	10.2	7.9	8.0	8.6	35.8
1991	4.1	6.9	4.3	9.4	8.2	8.9	8.5	37.7
1992	4.2	6.6	4.4	**8.6**	8.6	9.4	8.5	39.4
1993	4.4	6.3	5.1	8.3	9.4	9.9	9.3	41.0
1994	4.4	5.5	5.5	8.2	9.4	9.4	9.8	44.0
1995	4.3	5.2	5.5	8.8	9.4	9.5	9.9	39.7
1996	4.3	5.1	5.9	8.7	9.6	9.3	10.9	39.7
1997	4.5	5.0	6.4	8.1	9.8	9.7	11.0	41.6

Sources: Exports since 1993: *China Customs Statistics*, Economic Information &
Agency, Hong Kong; Guangdong's Exports from 1987–92: *The Statistics of
the External Economy, Trade and Tourism of the Guangdong Province*;
Guangdong Statistical Bureau, 1990, 1991, 1992; other statistics come from
the Shanghai, Guangdong and China *Statistics Yearbooks*.

Note: *China Customs Statistics* are used for Shanghai and Guangdong since 1993
and 1987 respectively (earliest available data), while MOFERT (Ministry of
Foreign Economic Relations and Trade) statistics, which are less accurate,
are used for previous years. MOFERT statistics greatly understate the
exports of Guangdong as a result of the importance of processing exports in
Guangdong (Sung, Liu, Wong, and Lau 1997: pp. 71–74). The problem does
not exist for Shanghai, as processing exports are insignificant there.

Guangdong and Shanghai is still very large. In a nutshell, despite the fact that China has shifted the focus of its developmental effort to Shanghai, Guangdong is still the premier region in China.

Investments of the China Circle

The investment flows among the trio, especially Hong Kong's investment in China, are very large. By the end of 1996 over 88% of Hong Kong's stock of outward FDI was in China, accounting for 57% of the stock of inward FDI in China. Largely as a result of Hong Kong's investment in China, China has become the foremost recipient of FDI among developing economies since 1992, and Hong Kong has become the foremost source of FDI among developing economies since 1991. Since 1993 China has been the second-largest recipient of FDI in the world, after the United States. From 1993 to 1996 Hong Kong was the world's fourth-largest source of FDI, after the United States, the United Kingdom, and Germany, but ahead of France and Japan. Figures for Hong Kong's investment in China are obtained from Chinese statistics, which include investment of the subsidiaries of multinationals in Hong Kong. (This is consistent with the international statistical practice that the source of investment should be attributed to the legal domicile of the firm.) Though such funds may originate elsewhere, the figures do show the importance of Hong Kong as a mediator of investment.

In 1995 Hong Kong's FDI in China was US$20 billion, or nearly three times the total inward FDI of US$7 billion in Mexico, which was the world's number two recipient of FDI among developing countries. Hong Kong's 1995 FDI in Guangdong province alone amounted to US$8 billion, exceeding the total inward FDI in Mexico. Taiwanese investment in China and China's investment in Hong Kong are also large, as will be detailed below.

Table 1.3 summarizes the FDI among China, Hong Kong, and Taiwan in a matrix. The first row shows the investments of China in Hong Kong, Taiwan, and the world. The second row shows the

Chapter 1

Table 1.3

**1996 Stock of Foreign Direct Investment (FDI)
within the Chinese Economic Area (CEA)
(US$ million)**

From	Investment Into				
	China	Hong Kong	Taiwan	CEA Total	World
China		14,766[1]		14,766	18,002
	—	(82.0)	—	(82.0)	(100)
		(18.7)		(5.5)	(0.56)
Hong Kong	99,297[2]		2,626[3]	101,923	112,156
	(88.5)	—	(2.3)	(90.9)	(100)
	(56.8)		(15.3)	(37.6)	(3.5)
Taiwan	15,734[2]	533[3]		16,267	27,296
	(57.6)	(2.0)	—	(59.6)	(100)
	(9.0)	(0.68)		(6.0)	(0.84)
CEA Total	**115,031**	**15,299**	**2,626**	**132,956**	**157,454**
	(73.1)	(9.7)	(1.7)	(84.4)	(100)
	(65.8)	(19.4)	(15.3)	(49.1)	(4.9)
World	174,884	78,782	17,138	270,804	3,233,228[*]
	(5.4)	(2.4)	(0.53)	(8.4)	—
	(100)	(100)	(100)	(100)	

Sources: All data come from the *World Investment Report 1996*, United Nations,
except the items below:

[1] *External Investments in Hong Kong's Non-manufacturing Sectors, 1996*,
Census and Statistics Department, Hong Kong, 1998.

[2] Table 2.5.

[3] See Chapter 6.

Note: Figures in upper brackets indicate percentage share of the row total; those
in lower brackets are column percentages.

[*] World Inward Foreign Direct Investment.

investments of Hong Kong in China, Taiwan, and the world, while
the third row shows the investments of Taiwan in China, Hong
Kong, and the world. The rows show the outward FDI of the
respective economies, while the columns show the inward FDI of
the respective economies.

Hong Kong's FDI in China is very large (row 2, column 1). The 1996 stock of Hong Kong's investment in China amounted to US$99.3 billion, which accounted for 57% of inward FDI in China or 88.5% of the stock of Hong Kong's outward FDI (the two percentages are shown in brackets beneath the figure of the stock of FDI).

China and Taiwan are also major investors. As a source of FDI among developing economies, Hong Kong has been the first since 1991, the Mainland was the second from 1992 to 1995, but slipped to the fifth from 1994 to 1996. Taiwan was first in 1990 (just ahead of Hong Kong), second to Hong Kong in 1991, and third, after Hong Kong and the Mainland, from 1992 to 1993. Taiwan slipped to the fourth from 1994 to 1996 (United Nations, 1997).

Taiwan's 1996 stock of FDI in China was US$ 15.7 billion (row 3, column 1). This accounts for 9.0% of China's inward FDI, or 57.6% of Taiwan's outward FDI. The Mainland was Taiwan's foremost destination of investment, and Taiwan was the second-largest investor in the Mainland, after Hong Kong. Mainland's 1996 stock of FDI in Hong Kong was US$14.8 billion (row 1, column 2), which was 18.7% of Hong Kong's inward FDI or 82% of China's outward FDI. Hong Kong has long been the foremost destination of China's investment, and the Mainland was the second largest investor in Hong Kong, after the United Kingdom.

Taiwan's 1996 stock of FDI in Hong Kong (row 3, column 2) was quite small (US$0.5 billion). However, Hong Kong's FDI in Taiwan (row 2, column 3) was sizeable, amounting to US$2.6 billion. This was 15% of Taiwan's inward FDI or 2% of Hong Kong's outward FDI. Hong Kong has been the third investor in Taiwan, after the United States and Japan, since the mid 1970s.

Intra-CEA FDI (row 4, column 4) was US$133 billion, which was 49% of the inward FDI of the CEA, and 84% of the outward FDI of the CEA. This shows that the CEA has invested mainly within itself, and around half of the FDI in CEA came from the CEA. In a nutshell, the CEA is highly integrated in terms of investment flows.

Chapter 1

Table 1.4
1997 Exports of the Chinese Economic Area (Official Statistics)
(US$ million)

From	China	Hong Kong	Taiwan	CEA Total	World
		Export To			
China	—	43,781 (24.0) (21.4)	3,396 (1.9) (3.1)	47,177 (25.8) (10.4)	182,697 (100) (3.4)
Hong Kong	65,583 (34.9) (47.0)	—	4,729 (2.5) (4.3)	70,312 (37.4) (15.4)	188,059 (100) (3.5)
Taiwan	—	28,708 (23.5) (14.0)	—	28,708 (23.5) (6.3)	122,081 (100) (2.3)
CEA Total	**65,583** (13.3) (47.0)	**72,489** (14.7) (35.4)	**8,125** (1.7) (7.3)	**146,197** (29.7) (32.1)	**492,837** (100) (9.2)
World	139,514 (2.6) (100)	204,859 (3.8) (100)	110,993 (2.1) (100)	455,366 (8.5) (100)	5,369,700 (100) (100)

Sources: China data come from *China Customs Statistics*; Hong Kong data: *Review of Overseas Trade*, Census and Statistics Department, Hong Kong, 1997; Taiwan data: *Monthly Bulletin of Statistics of the Republic of China* (see Table 1.1 for sources).

Note: Figures in upper brackets indicate percentage share of the row total; those in lower brackets are column percentages.

Trade of the Chinese Economic Area (CEA)

The investment flows of Hong Kong and Taiwan in China have generated huge trade flows. Fifty-four per cent of China's 1997 exports were produced in enterprises involving foreign investment (see Chapter 2 for details). As Hong Kong accounts for the bulk of foreign investment in China, it is no exaggeration to say that Hong Kong investment has been the backbone of China's spectacular export drive.

The trade flows generated by Hong Kong investment in Guangdong were huge. Since opening of China, most of Hong Kong's outward-processing activities in China were in Guangdong, and the bulk of their output was imported into Hong Kong for re-export to third countries. In 1996 the value of Hong Kong's re-export of goods made in Guangdong under outward-processing contracts was estimated to be nearly US$67.9 billion. This was 2.5 times the value of domestic exports of Hong Kong and also exceeded the value of Thailand's export of US$56.9 billion in the same year.

Table 1.4 shows the trade among the trio in matrix form. Official trade statistics are used to construct the Table. Row 1 shows China's exports to Hong Kong, Taiwan, the CEA, and the world, while column 1 shows exports to China from Hong Kong, Taiwan, the CEA, and the world. The world's exports to China are taken to be China's imports from the world less the cost of insurance and freight, which create a differential between the value of exports (in f.o.b. or "free on board" prices) and the value of imports (in c.i.f. or "cost, insurance, and freight" prices). A survey of the Hong Kong Government (Census and Statistics Department, Hong Kong, 1997b) found that the f.o.b. / c.i.f. ratio for Hong Kong was 0.982 in 1996, and the ratio was applied to Hong Kong's imports in 1997. As expected, the ratio for land transport (0.991) was higher than that for ocean (0.973), and the ratio for Asia (0.986) was higher than that for more distant partners such as those in North America (0.959). As Taiwan depends exclusively on ocean transport for its trade, its ratio was taken to be 0.97. Mainland's ratio should be close to Hong Kong's because Hong Kong is China's foremost trading partner. China's ratio was taken to be 0.98. Row 5 thus shows world exports to the respective economies, or, more simply, imports of the respective economies in f.o.b. prices.

Complications of Trade Statistics

China's 1997 exports to Hong Kong (row 1, column 2) were US$43.8 billion, which was 24% of China's exports or 21.4% of

Hong Kong's imports in f.o.b. prices (The two percentages are shown in brackets beneath the figure of China's exports to Hong Kong.) According to China's official statistics, Hong Kong is the foremost market for Chinese exports.

However, China's statistics on exports to Hong Kong are biased upwards, and China's exports to other economies are biased downwards, because a substantial portion of Chinese exports to Hong Kong are re-exported to third economies (including Taiwan). To obtain an accurate picture of trade among the CEA, adjustments for China's trade via Hong Kong with third economies must be made.

In trade statistics, there are the following three ways of classifying trade by region:

1. Both imports and exports are classified by region of consignment.
2. Imports are classified by region of origin, whereas exports are classified by region of consignment.
3. Imports are classified by region of origin, whereas exports are classified by region of final destination.

The first classification is the easiest to implement, as information on the region of consignment is easily obtainable. Most economies have adopted the second classification, as tariffs and quotas often depend on the region of origin. The third classification is theoretically useful but is difficult to implement, as most economies cannot ascertain the final destination of their exports. For instance, it is not easy for China to trace accurately the ultimate destination of Hong Kong's re-exports of Chinese goods to third economies, simply because Hong Kong traders who have bought Chinese products are free to sell them to any country.

Up to 1992 China's trade statistics supposedly followed the second classification, which is the usual international practice. However, part of Hong Kong's re-exports of third-country goods to China were recorded in Chinese statistics as imports from Hong Kong, as China had not been able to ascertain the true origin of the vast amounts of third-country products imported through Hong

Kong. China's statistics on trade with Hong Kong were inflated in two ways. First, China's imports from Hong Kong included part of Hong Kong's re-exports of third-country goods to China. Second, China's exports to Hong Kong included all goods re-exported via Hong Kong to third economies. It is not surprising that China regarded Hong Kong as both its foremost market and its foremost supplier in 1992.

As a result of the vast amount of China's trade with third countries via Hong Kong, statistics on China's bilateral trade are highly inaccurate. For instance, in United States–China trade, both countries regard their exports to each other through Hong Kong as exports to Hong Kong, thereby understating exports to each other. Imports are not understated, as they are traced to the country of origin.[2] Both countries thus overstate their bilateral trade deficits or understate their bilateral surpluses. For example, in 1992 U.S. statistics claimed a deficit of US$18 billion in the United States' trade with China, whereas China claimed a trade deficit of US$306 million with the United States. However, U.S. statistics are less misleading than those of China, because in the early 1990s around two-thirds of China's exports to the United States were re-exported through Hong Kong, whereas the corresponding ratio of the United States' exports was only around 20%.

Because of U.S. pressure, China tried to trace the final destination of its exports via Hong Kong, and a substantial portion of its exports to Hong Kong were re-classified as exports to final destinations in 1993. As a result, China's exports to Hong Kong dropped by 41%, and its exports to the United States, Japan, and Germany increased by 97%, 35%, and 62%, respectively, in 1993. Despite the reclassification, a substantial portion of China's exports via Hong Kong to third countries are still classified as exports to Hong Kong, because China is unable to trace the final destination of all of its exports via Hong Kong, and Hong Kong remains the foremost market for Chinese exports.

Since 1993 China has some success in classifying its imports by origin, and its imports from Hong Kong no longer include Hong Kong's re-exports of third economies to China. As a result, Hong

Table 1.5

1997 Exports of the Chinese Economic Area by Region of Consignment (US$ million)

From	China	Hong Kong	Taiwan	CEA Total	World
		Consignment To			
China		74,442	2,838	77,280	182,697
	—	(40.8)	(1.6)	(42.3)	(100)
		(36.3)	(2.6)	(17.0)	(3.4)
Hong Kong	65,583		4,729	70,312	188,059
	(34.9)	—	(2.5)	(37.4)	(100)
	(47.0)		(4.3)	(15.4)	(3.5)
Taiwan		28,708		28,708	122,081
	—	(23.5)	—	(23.5)	(100)
		(14.0)		(6.3)	(2.3)
CEA Total	**65,583**	**103,150**	**7,567**	**176,300**	**492,837**
	(13.3)	(20.9)	(1.5)	(35.8)	(100)
	(47.0)	(50.4)	(6.8)	(38.7)	(9.2)
World	139,514	204,859	110,993	455,366	5,369,700
	(2.6)	(3.8)	(2.1)	(8.5)	(100)
	(100)	(100)	(100)	(100)	(100)

Sources: China data come from Tables 4.2 and 6.3; Hong Kong and Taiwan data: Table 1.4.

Note: Figures in upper brackets indicate percentage share of the row total; those in lower brackets are column percentages.

Kong became the fourth supplier of imports to China in 1993 (after Japan, Taiwan, and the United States) instead of the first.

This book will use mainly Hong Kong statistics in the discussion on Hong Kong–China trade, because China's statistics fail to distinguish between China's trade with third countries via Hong Kong and China's trade with Hong Kong itself. Chinese statistics on trade by region are also inconsistent over time as a result of the 1993 reclassification. Hong Kong trade statistics carefully distinguish between re-exports and domestic exports (exports of goods made domestically), and it is possible to accurately estimate China's trade with Hong Kong, Taiwan, and other economies by using Hong

Kong data on the re-export of Chinese goods. The estimation of China's trade with Hong Kong is discussed in detail in Chapter 4.

Re-examination of Trade in the CEA

Given the foregoing discussion of trade statistics, three alternative matrices showing trade in the CEA appear in Tables 1.5 to 1.7. Table 1.5 shows exports of the CEA by region of consignment (first classification), Table 1.6 shows domestic exports of the CEA by region of consignment (second classification), and Table 1.7 shows domestic exports of the CEA by region of final destination (third classification).

In Table 1.5 the 1997 value of exports of China consigned to Hong Kong (including all of China's exports via Hong Kong to third economies) was US$74.4 billion, which was 41% of the value of China's exports and 36% of the value of China's imports (in f.o.b. prices). This figure is much larger than the US$43.8 billion figure in Table 1.4, which, as a result of the 1993 reclassification, only includes part of China's exports via Hong Kong.

In Table 1.5 the value of 1997 exports of China consigned to Taiwan was US$ 2.8 billion — less than the figure of US$ 3.4 billion in Table 1.4. This is because the figure in Table 1.4 includes some exports to Taiwan consigned via Hong Kong.

The second and third rows in Tables 1.4 and 1.5 are the same (exports of Hong Kong and Taiwan). This is because Hong Kong and Taiwan report their exports by region of consignment. Hong Kong's 1997 exports to China were valued at US$65.6 billion — 35% of Hong Kong's exports and 47% of Hong Kong's imports (in f.o.b. prices). China and Hong Kong were each other's foremost market and foremost supplier.

Taiwan's 1997 exports to Hong Kong were valued at US$28.7 billion — 23% of Taiwan's exports and 14% of Hong Kong's imports (in f.o.b. prices). Hong Kong was the second-largest market for Taiwan, after the United States. According to Taiwan's statistics, there were no exports of Taiwan to China, because the bulk of Taiwan's exports to China were consigned via Hong Kong.

Chapter 1

Table 1.6
1997 Domestic Exports of the Chinese Economic Area
by Region of Consignment
(US$ million)

		Consignment To			
From	China	Hong Kong	Taiwan	CEA Total	World
China		74,442	2,838	77,280	182,697
	—	(40.8)	(1.6)	(42.3)	(100)
		(36.3)	(2.6)	(17.0)	(3.4)
Hong Kong	8,249		908	9,157	27,307
	(30.2)	—	(3.3)	(33.5)	(100)
	(5.9)		(0.8)	(2.0)	(0.5)
Taiwan		28,708		28,708	122,801
	—	(23.5)	—	(23.5)	(100)
		(14.0)		(6.3)	(2.3)
CEA Total	**8,249**	**103,150**	**3,746**	**115,145**	**332,085**
	(2.5)	(31.1)	(1.1)	(34.7)	(100)
	(5.9)	(50.4)	(3.4)	(25.3)	(6.2)
World	139,514	204,859	110,993	455,366	5,369,700
	(2.6)	(3.8)	(2.1)	(8.5)	(100)
	(100)	(100)	(100)	(100)	(100)

Sources: China & Taiwan data come from Table 1.5; Hong Kong data: *Review of Overseas trade* (see Table 1.4 for source).

Note: Figures in upper brackets indicate percentage share of the row total; those in lower brackets are column percentages.

Table 1.5 shows that intra-CEA exports (column 4) of China, Hong Kong, and Taiwan were 42%, 37%, and 23% of their respective exports. The total value of intra-CEA exports (column 4, row 4) was US$176 billion — 36% of CEA exports or 39% of CEA imports (in f.o.b. prices). Trade in the CEA shows a substantial degree of integration.

However, Table 1.5 exaggerates the integration of trade in the CEA for two reasons. First, the table is based on region of consignment instead of on final destination, and the bulk of China's exports consigned to Hong Kong were re-exported to non-CEA destinations. Second, the bulk of Hong Kong's exports were re-exports of

Table 1.7
1997 Domestic Exports of the Chinese Economic Area by Final Destination
(US$ million)

From	Export To				
	China	Hong Kong	Taiwan	CEA Total	World
China		5,670	4,377	10,047	182,697
	—	(3.1)	(2.4)	(5.5)	(100)
		(7.6)	(3.9)	(3.1)	(3.4)
Hong Kong	8,249		908	9,157	27,307
	(30.2)	—	(3.3)	(33.5)	(100)
	(5.9)		(0.8)	(2.8)	(0.51)
Taiwan	21,965	5,836		27,801	122,081
	(18.0)	(4.8)	—	(22.8)	(100)
	(15.7)	(7.8)		(8.6)	(2.3)
CEA Total	**30,214**	**11,506**	**5,285**	**47,005**	**332,085**
	(9.1)	(3.5)	(1.6)	(14.2)	(100)
	(21.7)	(15.4)	(4.8)	(14.4)	(6.2)
World	139,514	74,828	110,993	325,335	5,369,700
	(2.6)	(1.4)	(2.1)	(6.1)	(100)
	(100)	(100)	(100)	(100)	(100)

Sources: China data come from Tables 4.2 and 6.3; Hong Kong data: *Review of Overseas Trade* (see Table 1.4 for source); Taiwan data: Tables 6.1 and 6.2.

Note: Figures in upper brackets indicate percentage share of the row total; those in lower brackets are column percentages.

non-Hong Kong goods, including a substantial amount of Chinese goods. There is thus double counting in Table 1.5. For instance, Hong Kong's exports to Taiwan overlap with China's exports to Hong Kong because part of China's exports to Hong Kong were re-exported to Taiwan.

Table 1.6 eliminates the second problem, while Table 1.7 eliminates both problems. Row 2 of Table 1.6 shows the domestic exports of Hong Kong by region of consignment, excluding all re-exports. Rows 1 and 3 (exports of China and Taiwan by region of consignment) are the same as those in Table 1.5, as the exports of

China and Taiwan are mostly local products. The columns of Table 1.6 show imports by region of origin (second classification), as re-exports are excluded.

Table 1.6 shows that intra-CEA trade was 35% of CEA exports and 25% of CEA imports (row 4, column 4). This is still biased upwards. Though there is no double counting in Table 1.6, China's exports to the CEA are still exaggerated because the bulk of China's exports consigned to Hong Kong are re-exported to non-CEA destination.

Table 1.7 eliminates all biases and shows the domestic exports of the CEA by final destination (third classification). The bulk of the exports of China and Taiwan to Hong Kong are re-exported elsewhere, and such re-exports are accordingly deducted.

Row 1 shows China's exports. The value of China's exports consumed in Hong Kong was only US$5.7 billion — 3.1% of China's exports and 7.6% of Hong Kong's retained imports (imports consumed in Hong Kong) in f.o.b. prices. Unlike in the 1960s, Hong Kong was no longer an important final market for China. With rapid economic growth in Hong Kong, Hong Kong consumers have shifted to high-quality consumer goods (automobiles, high-fidelity audio equipment) produced by Japan. China's 1997 exports to Taiwan were valued at US$4.4 billion — 2.4% of China's exports or 3.9% of Taiwan's imports (in f.o.b. prices). China's exports to Taiwan were few partly because of Taiwan's controls on imports of mainland products. The CEA only accounted for 5.5% of China's exports by final destination.

Row 2 shows that Hong Kong's 1997 domestic exports to China were valued at US$8 billion — 30% of the value Hong Kong's domestic exports or 5.9% of that of China's imports. China surpassed the United States as the foremost market for Hong Kong products in 1993. In 1997, Hong Kong was the fifth supplier of China, after Japan, Taiwan, the United States, and South Korea. The amount of Hong Kong's domestic exports to Taiwan was small.

Row 3 shows that Taiwan's 1997 exports to China were valued at US$22 billion – 18% of the value of Taiwan's exports and nearly

16% of the value of China's imports (in f.o.b. prices). China was the number two market for Taiwan, after the United States, and Taiwan was the number two supplier of China, after Japan. Taiwan and Hong Kong together supplied nearly 22% of China's 1997 imports (in f.o.b. prices). Taiwan's 1997 exports consumed in Hong Kong were valued at US$ 5.8 billion — 4.8% of Taiwan's exports and 7.8% of Hong Kong's retained imports. Hong Kong was the fourth market for Taiwan, after the United States, China, and Japan. Taiwan was the third supplier of Hong Kong retained imports (in f.o.b. prices), after Japan and the United States.

Intra-CEA 1997 exports were valued at US$47 billion — only 14% of the value of exports and imports of the CEA. The degree of the integration of the CEA in term of trade flows is much lower than that in terms of FDI. This is because Hong Kong and Taiwan investors use the Mainland as a platform to manufacture labour-intensive products for non-CEA markets, mostly the United States and the European Union. Ninety-four per cent of China's 1996 exports were for non-CEA markets.

Hong Kong and Taiwan supply China with semi-manufactured goods, which are further processed in China for export to the United States and the European Union. China is thus an important market for Hong Kong and Taiwan, and the latter two economies are important suppliers of China. However, if we net out the flow of semi-manufactured goods between Hong Kong and China and only look at the flow of final products, the United States and the European Union are still the foremost markets for Hong Kong products (see Chapter 4).

The economic reality of the trio is that the United States is their largest market, and Japan is their largest supplier of capital goods and technology. An inward-looking bloc of the trio excluding the United States and Japan would not be in the trio's long-term interest.

In the long run, China will liberalize its imports of consumer goods and will import more consumer goods relative to semi-manufactured ones. China will likely shift its imports away from Taiwan and Hong Kong to Japan and the West. Taiwan and Hong

Table 1.8
Exports of the Chinese Economic Area (CEA):
Position among Leading World Exporters, 1996

Exporter	Exports (US$ billion)	Position in 1996
United States	625	1
Germany	521	2
Japan	413	3
France	290	4
United Kingdom	259	5
Italy	251	6
Canada	201	7
Netherlands	197	8
Hong Kong	181	9
Belgium Luxemberg	167	10
China	151	11
Korea (Republic of)	130	12
Singapore	125	13
Taiwan	116	14
Spain	102	15
Mexico	96	16
Sweden	84	17
CEA (Gross)	**449**	**(3)**
CEA goods*	254	(6)
HK–Guangdong goods*	90	(17)

Source: World Trade Organization.

Note: * See text for method of estimation. Numbers in brackets are hypothetical
             rankings.

Kong cannot remain important suppliers of China for long, because
their industrial bases are quite narrow. However, it is likely that
China will remain an important market for Hong Kong and Taiwan
because of the sheer size of the Chinese economy. China has to look
outside the CEA for its capital goods, technology, and market. The
liberalization of China's imports will imply rich opportunities for
East Asia and the world.

Exports of the China Circle in the International Context

The Chinese Economic Area is a large exporter. Table 1.8 shows the exports of the China Circle in the international context. In 1996 Hong Kong, the Mainland, and Taiwan were, respectively, the world's ninth, eleventh, and fourteenth exporters. The total value of exports of the China Circle was US$449 billion, which was the third in the world, surpassing Japan's exports, which were valued at US$413 billion.

However, adding up the exports of the China Circle exaggerates its exports for two reasons. First, the bulk of Hong Kong's exports consist of re-exports that are not made in Hong Kong. To gauge the capacity of the Hong Kong economy to manufacture goods for export, domestic exports rather than total exports should be the relevant measure. After deducting Hong Kong's re-exports, the exports of the CEA should valued at US$294 billion.

Second, we should deduct intra-CEA exports, the value of which amounted to US$41 billion. The adjusted 1996 exports of the CEA were valued at US$254 billion — the sixth in the world, after the United Kingdom but ahead of Italy. It is clear that the CEA is a very large exporter.

In 1996 the domestic exports of Hong Kong–Guangdong were valued at US$90 billion — the seventeenth in the world. Hong Kong–Guangdong is also a large exporter.

Organization of the Book

Following this introductory chapter, Chapter 2 will analyze the opening of China and the economic integration of the China Circle. Chapter 3 will cover the policy changes among the trio that led to the reintegration of Greater South China. Chapters 4 and 5 will cover, respectively, trade and investment between Hong Kong and

China, especially Guangdong. Chapter 6 will cover trade and investment between Taiwan and China, and between Taiwan and Hong Kong. Chapter 7 will cover policy issues, and Chapter 8 will conclude with a discussion of the problems and prospects of the China Circle.

Notes

1. The term "natural economic territory" was coined by Robert A. Scalapino in "The United States and Asia: Future Prospects," *Foreign Affairs* 70, no. 5 (Winter 1991–92): pp. 19–40.

2. China's imports from the United States might have been slightly understated, as some of them might be recorded as imports from Hong Kong. The understatement is, however, not serious, as U.S. exports to China via Hong Kong were quite small.

CHAPTER 2

China's Opening and the Economic Integration of the China Circle

China's Opening and Economic Reform

As China's opening is the crux to the integration of the CEA, this chapter will briefly summarize the main features of this opening.[1] Before China's 1979 reforms, its centrally planned economy was designed to insulate its economy from the world market so that planners could administer the domestic economy according to their priorities. To raise savings and investment and to depress consumption, China fixed wages and the price of agricultural products at levels much lower than those of the world market, so peasants had little income. At the same time, the prices of manufactured consumer goods were fixed at levels much higher than those of the world market to ensure that peasants could not buy much with their meagre income. The state could thus squeeze out a huge surplus for investment and national defence.

To preserve China's artificial price structure, which was very different from that of the world market, planners had to insulate the domestic economy from the world market through a state monopoly on foreign trade and also through foreign exchange controls. Otherwise, Chinese enterprises would have been able to trade freely, Chinese price levels would have converged to world market levels, and central planning would have failed. China's exports and imports had to be centrally administered, and the process was, understandably, inefficient.

Centrally planned economies do not trade much. With their highly centralized foreign trade systems, they find it difficult to participate in international trade. Trade is reduced to a minimum. Imports are confined to indispensable goods that are not available domestically, and planners have to squeeze out some commodities for exports to earn enough foreign exchange for imports. Trade is regarded as a necessary evil.

In contrast, foreign trade has been the engine of growth for many newly industrializing economies including Hong Kong, Taiwan, Singapore, and South Korea. In these economies, foreign trade is a potent channel of technology transfer. Exporters learn to master state-of-the-art technology through competition in the world market. Domestic producers are forced to become efficient to match the standards of imports produced by efficient producers overseas.

A centrally planned economy forgoes many of the benefits of trade. Domestic producers lose sight of international standards, as they do not have to compete with imports. Moreover, foreign trade is monopolized and handled by state foreign trade corporations. Producers are compelled by the state plan to deliver their products to these corporations for export. Producers thus do not have direct contact with foreign buyers. This implies that domestic producers have little chance to learn about international practices and standards. Users of imports (e.g., enterprises using imported machinery) have to apply for allocation of imports from the state, and they do not have direct contact with foreign suppliers. This implies that state foreign trade corporations may easily import the wrong equipment for the end users.

In the pre-reform era China was able to build a huge industrial system through forced savings. However, the greater part of the Chinese industrial system was highly inefficient and technologically backward. China's opening to foreign trade and investment has been essential to the country's reform.

China's opening has involved the gradual abolition of the state monopoly on foreign trade through decentralizing the power to trade to a larger number of entities, including ministerial and provincial trading corporations, large enterprises, and enterprises operated by foreign investors. It has entailed the progressive relaxation of foreign exchange controls and the freeing of the exchange rate so that foreign trade would be co-ordinated by market forces instead of by central planning. It has also involved the creation of an environment friendly to foreign investment through the establishment of Special Economic Zones (SEZs) and open areas with special privileges for foreign investors, as well as through the enactment of legislation protecting their rights.

Despite setbacks, detours, and unresolved problems, China's open policy has been extraordinarily successful. From 1979 to 1997 China's rank as an exporter in the world jumped from thirty-second to eleventh. Inward FDI soared. China has been by far the largest recipient of FDI among developing countries since 1992 and has been second only to the United States in the world since 1993. As a source of FDI, China was the second-largest among developing economies, after Hong Kong, from 1992 to 1993, and the fifth largest, after Hong Kong, Singapore, South Korea, and Taiwan from 1994 to 1996.

China tailored its opening toward Hong Kong, Macau, and Taiwan. In 1979 Beijing gave Guangdong and Fujian special policy packages that vastly increased their autonomy, including the management of foreign trade and investment and the authority to operate SEZs. Guangdong operates three SEZs: the Shenzhen and Zhuhai SEZs adjacent to Hong Kong and Macao respectively, and the Shantou SEZ, which has close links to overseas Chinese populations and a community in Hong Kong that originated in Shantou. Fujian operates the Xiamen SEZ opposite Taiwan.

The opening of China coincided with the emergence of labour shortages in Hong Kong and Taiwan and the latter two economies' need to restructure. The export-oriented, labour-intensive industries of Hong Kong moved to Guangdong on a large scale, while labour-intensive industries in Taiwan similarly moved to Guangdong and Fujian. The economic integration of the CEA started with export-oriented labour-intensive industries and have by now moved to other sectors such as infrastructure and services.

Categorization of Foreign Investment

Foreign investment, especially the investment of Hong Kong and Taiwan in the Mainland, plays a vital role in the economic integration of the CEA. Chinese statistics on foreign investment distinguish between "contracted investment" and "utilized investment". The former is better for gauging the intention to invest, while the latter is a better measurement of the actual size of the investment flow.

The categorization of various types of foreign capital inflow can be quite confusing. This book adopts the following classification:

1. Loans and other forms of indirect investment
2. Foreign investment
   a. Foreign Direct Investment (FDI)
      (i) Wholly foreign-owned ventures
      (ii) Joint ventures
      (iii) Co-operative ventures
   b. Other Foreign Investment: Processing / assembling[2]

Loans are a form of indirect investment, as the foreign investor has no control of the enterprises involved, whereas the investor has legal control in the case of foreign direct investment (e.g., equity ownership). FDI includes investment in the "three types of foreign-funded enterprises" (*sanzi qiye*, namely, fully foreign-owned ventures, joint ventures, and co-operative ventures). The most important form of "other foreign investment" is processing/assembling operations, referred to as processing operations for brevity. In processing operations, Chinese firms process raw materials supplied by foreign firms for a processing fee. The processed outputs belong to the foreign firms and are exported by them. The foreign firms usually provide the required machinery, product design, and technical assistance. "Other foreign investment" constitutes commercial credit rather than FDI, because the Chinese partner legally controls the operation and usually pays for foreign machinery and technical assistance with labour services used in making goods under contract for the foreign partner.

Despite the legal distinction, the nature of "other foreign investment" is similar to that of FDI, as foreign machinery and technology is made available for the use of the Chinese partner. Moreover, the foreign partner often has de facto control over the operation. In this article, the term "foreign investment" includes both FDI and "other foreign investment" but excludes loans.

Foreign Capital in China

Tables 2.1 and 2.2 show, respectively, contracted and utilized foreign capital in China. Utilized foreign loans exceeded FDI until 1991. Deng's 1992 southern tour in support of economic reforms led to a big jump in FDI, and utilized loans constituted only 9.6% of utilized foreign capital in 1997.

Our analysis focuses on FDI rather than on loans for three reasons. First, loans are of decreasing importance in China's utilization of foreign capital. Second, in comparison with foreign investment, loans represent more of an arm's-length relationship and are less potent for technology transfer. Third, loans are not a very good indicator of the investment environment, because a substantial portion of foreign loans to China are official loans, which may be given on non-economic grounds.

Contracted FDI is more volatile than utilized FDI because the former is sensitive to expectations of changes in the investment environment. Utilized FDI increased steadily from the early 1980s to 1989, stagnated from 1989 to 1990 because of the Tiananmen incident, and then jumped upwards in 1992 as a result of Deng's southern tour.

Contracted FDI rose rapidly in the early 1980's to a peak in 1985, reflecting euphoria over the China market during the initial stage of China's opening. However, the euphoria evaporated with the many problems of the Chinese investment environment, and contracted FDI tumbled in 1986. The reversal disturbed the Chinese leadership, which announced a twenty-two-point investment

Table 2.1
Contracted Foreign Capital in China, 1979–97
(US$ million)

	Total	Foreign Loans	Foreign Direct Investment	Other Foreign Investment	
				Subtotal	Processing Operations
1979–83	23,978	15,062	7,742	1,174	279
	(100)	(62.8)	(32.3)	(4.9)	(1.2)
1984	4,791	1,916	2,651	224	63
	(100)	(40.0)	(55.3)	(4.7)	(1.3)
1985	9,867	3,534	5,932	401	98
	(100)	(35.8)	(60.1)	(4.1)	(0.99)
1986	11,737	8,407	2,843	496	140
	(100)	(71.6)	(24.2)	(4.2)	(1.2)
1987	12,136	7,817	3,709	610	165
	(100)	(64.4)	(30.6)	(5.0)	(1.4)
1988	16,004	9,813	5,297	894	205
	(100)	(61.3)	(33.1)	(5.6)	(1.3)
1989	11,479	5,185	5,600	694	148
	(100)	(45.2)	(48.8)	(6.0)	(1.3)
1990	12,086	5,099	6,596	391	136
	(100)	(42.2)	(54.6)	(3.2)	(1.1)
1991	19,583	7,161	11,977	445	148
	(100)	(36.6)	(61.2)	(2.3)	(0.76)
1992	69,439	10,703	58,124	612	120
	(100)	(15.4)	(83.7)	(0.88)	(0.17)
1993	123,273	11,306	111,436	531	196
	(100)	(9.2)	(90.4)	(0.43)	(0.16)
1994	93,756	10,668	82,680	408	196
	(100)	(11.4)	(88.2)	(0.44)	(0.21)
1995	103,205	11,288	91,282	635	189
	(100)	(10.9)	(88.4)	(0.62)	(0.18)
1996	81,609	7,962	73,276	371	209
	(100)	(9.8)	(89.8)	(0.45)-	(0.26)
1979–96	592,943	115,921	469,136	7,886	2,292
	(100)	(19.6)	(79.1)	(1.3)	(0.39)
1997	61,058	5,872	51,003	4,183	1,696
	(100)	(9.6)	(83.5)	(6.9)	(2.8)
1979–97	654,001	121,793	520,139	12,069	3,988
	(100)	(18.6)	(79.5)	(1.8)	(0.61)

Source: *Almanac of China's Foreign Relations and Trade*, various issues.
Note: Figures in brackets are row percentages.

Table 2.2
Utilized Foreign Capital in China, 1979–97
(US$ million)

Year	Total	Foreign Loans	Foreign Direct Investment	Other Foreign Investment	
				Subtotal	Processing Operations
1979–83	14,438	11,755	1,802	881	316
	(100)	(81.4)	(12.5)	(6.1)	(2.2)
1984	2,705	1,286	1,258	161	63
	(100)	(47.5)	(46.5)	(6.0)	(2.3)
1985	4,647	2,688	1,661	298	98
	(100)	(57.8)	(35.7)	(6.4)	(2.1)
1986	7,258	5,014	1,874	370	140
	(100)	(69.1)	(25.8)	(5.1)	(1.9)
1987	8,452	5,805	2,314	333	91
	(100)	(68.7)	(27.4)	(3.9)	(1.1)
1988	10,226	6,487	3,194	545	69
	(100)	(63.4)	(31.2)	(5.3)	(0.67)
1989	10,059	6,286	3,392	381	56
	(100)	(62.5)	(33.7)	(3.8)	(0.56)
1990	10,289	6,534	3,487	268	79
	(100)	(63.5)	(33.9)	(2.6)	(0.77)
1991	11,554	6,888	4,366	300	85
	(100)	(59.6)	(37.8)	(2.6)	(0.74)
1992	19,202	7,911	11,007	284	67
	(100)	(41.2)	(57.3)	(1.5)	(0.35)
1993	38,960	11,189	27,515	256	120
	(100)	(28.7)	(70.6)	(0.66)	(0.31)
1994	43,213	9,267	33,767	179	71
	(100)	(21.4)	(78.1)	(0.41)	(0.16)
1995	48,133	10,327	37,521	285	44
	(100)	(21.5)	(78.0)	(0.59)	(0.91)
1996	54,804	12,669	41,726	409	164
	(100)	(23.1)	(76.1)	(0.75)	(0.30)
1979–96	283,940	104,106	174,884	4,950	1,463
	(100)	(36.7)	(61.6)	(1.7)	(0.52)
1997	64,408	12,021	45,257	7,130	1,070
	(100)	(18.7)	(70.3)	(11.1)	(1.7)
1979–97	348,348	116,127	220,141	12,080	2,533
	(100)	(33.3)	(63.2)	(3.5)	(0.7)

Source: *Almanac of China's Foreign Relations and Trade*, various issues.
Note: Figures in brackets are row percentages.

Table 2.3
Contracted Foreign Capital by Industry, 1979–96
(US$ million)

Year	Total	Agriculture	Industry	Oil Develop- ment	Real Estate	Others
1979–85	12,130	222	4,282	1,397	2,271	4,138
	(100)	(1.8)	(35.3)	(11.5)	(18.7)	(32.7)
1986	2,834	62	785	n.a.	1,617	370
	(100)	(2.2)	(27.7)		(57.1)	(13.0)
1987	3,709	125	1,776	n.a.	1,471	337
	(100)	(3.4)	(47.9)		(39.7)	(9.0)
1988	5,297	209	4,021	2	530	535
	(100)	(3.9)	(75.9)	(0.0)	(10.0)	(10.2)
1989	5,600	121	4,664	n.a.	524	291
	(100)	(2.2)	(83.3)		(9.4)	(5.1)
1990	6,596	122	5,569	0	452	453
	(100)	(1.8)	(84.4)	(0.0)	(6.9)	(6.9)
1991	11,977	220	9,623	n.a.	1,504	630
	(100)	(1.8)	(80.3)		(12.6)	(5.3)
1992	58,124	678	32,667	3	18,080	6,696
	(100)	(1.2)	(56.2)	(0.0)	(31.1)	(11.5)
1993	111,436	1,191	51,174	81	43,771	15,219
	(100)	(1.1)	(45.9)	(0.1)	(39.3)	(13.6)
1994	82,680	972	43,899	54	23,862	13,893
	(100)	(1.2)	(53.1)	(0.1)	(28.9)	(16.7)
1995	91,282	1,736	61,648	12	17,835	10,051
	(100)	(1.9)	(67.5)	(0.0)	(19.5)	(11.1)
1979–95	391,665	4,797	199,011	150	105,052	82,655
	(100)	(1.4)	(56.2)	(0.4)	(28.6)	(13.4)
1996	81,610	1,412	51,607	13	12,851	15,727
	(100)	(1.7)	(63.2)	(0.02)	(15.8)	(19.28)
1979–96	473,275	6,209	250,618	163	117,903	98,382
	(100)	(1.3)	(53.0)	(0.03)	(24.9)	(20.77)

Source: *Almanac of China's Foreign Relations and Trade*, various issues.
Note: Figures in brackets are row percentages.

enticement package in October 1986 (Sung 1991, p. 56) that led to a rise in contracted FDI from 1987 onwards. Contracted FDI jumped nearly five time in 1992, reflecting the effect of Deng's southern tour.

The impact of the Tiananmen incident on contracted FDI was masked because it occurred in the middle of the year: the excellent record in the first half of 1989 helped to make up for a dismal performance in the second half. Moreover, contracted FDI from Hong Kong and Taiwan held up despite a dramatic fall in FDI from western countries.

From 1991 to 1992 utilized FDI in China jumped from US$4.4 billion to US$11 billion, and China became by far the largest recipient of FDI among developing countries, with a 22% share of the total. China's utilized FDI in 1994, 1995, 1996 and 1997 was US$33.8 billion (+23%), US$37.5 billion (+11%), US$41.7 billion (+11%), and US$45.3 billion (+8.5%) respectively, accounting for close to 40% of total FDI in developing countries. From 1993 to 1997 FDI in China by far exceeded the FDI in the entire Association of South-East Asian Nations (ASEAN), and China was second only to the United States in the world in inward FDI.

Despite the continuing rise in utilized FDI, contracted FDI has been beneath the 1993 peak (US$111.4 billion) for the four consecutive years of 1994 (US$82.7 billion), 1995 (US$91.3 billion), 1996 (US$73.3 billion) and 1997 (US$510 billion). Since contracted FDI signals future trends, China's annual inward utilized FDI has probably peaked. As East Asian economies, which are the main sources of China's inward FDI, have suffered from the East Asian financial crisis, inward utilized FDI is forecasted to drop sharply in 1998.

Table 2.3 shows the distribution of contracted foreign capital by industry (the distribution of FDI by industry is not available). Industry and real estate accounted for, respectively, 53% and 25% of cumulative contracted foreign capital from 1979 to 1996. The two sectors together accounted for 78% of contracted foreign capital, and the shares of other sectors were quite small.

From 1979 to 1985 the share of industry was smaller (35.3%), as Hong Kong's manufacturers did not relocate to China on a large scale until 1986, when the labour shortage in Hong Kong became severe. The share of oil development was substantial (11.5%) as oil companies were attracted to China by the prospect of discovering oil in the South China Sea. However, the oil strikes were disappointing, and foreign capital in oil development dwindled.

Real estate's share fluctuated with the bubbles of the real estate market. There was a bubble in 1986 and 1986, and real estate's share in contracted foreign capital was 57.1% and 39.7%, respectively. Industry share decreased correspondingly. Real estate's share fell to around 10% or lower from 1988 to 1991, and industry's share rose to close to 80% or above. Deng's 1992 tour led to another real estate boom, and real estate's share rose to close to 30% or more from 1992 to 1994. However, with macrostabilization starting in mid-1994, its share fell to 15.8% in 1996.

China as an Export Base and as a Market

Two ideal types of investment projects can be distinguished: the first utilizing China as an export base and the second establishing a presence in China's domestic markets. The first type of project tends to involve small-scale, labour-intensive manufacturing, while the second type tends to be large and more capital or technology intensive, involving manufacturing as well as services, which usually cannot be exported. Historically, Hong Kong and Taiwan have invested in the first type of project, whereas developed countries such as the United States and Japan seem to have concentrated their investment in the second type. With the gradual opening of China's domestic market after Deng's 1992 southern tour, Hong Kong and Taiwan have increasingly invested in the second type of project, as well.

It happens that the two types of projects fall roughly into two different categories in China's statistics on foreign investment. The first type correspond to processing operations that are export oriented by definition (they have to export their entire output) and tend to be labour intensive. The second correspond to foreign-invested enterprises, as they can sell part of their output in the domestic market and tend to be larger in scale and more capital intensive. However, the distinction between the two is not sharp, as many foreign-invested enterprises also process imported materials for export under contract. The bulk of exports from foreign-invested enterprises (77% in 1997) are processed exports. Instead of earning a processing fee, as in the case of processing operations, foreign-invested enterprises own their output and sell the processed exports for a profit.

As processing operations are labour rather than capital intensive, their contribution to capital formation is quite small. In 1997, utilized investment in processing operations was only 1.7% of utilized foreign capital in China (Table 2.2).[3] However, processing operations are important in China's exports, as they are completely export oriented. Of China's 1997 exports, 13% were exports from processing operations and 41% were exports from foreign-invested enterprises. Foreign investment thus accounted for a total of 54% of China's exports. As Hong Kong and Taiwan account for the bulk of foreign investment in processing operations and also in exported-oriented foreign-invested enterprises, the investment from the two economies are vital to China's spectacular export drive.

Foreign Investment in China by Source

Tables 2.4 and 2.5 show, respectively, China's contracted and utilized FDI by source. Hong Kong is by far the largest investor in China, Taiwan is a distant second, and the United States and Japan vie for the third place respectively. Hong Kong's share of both contracted and utilized FDI in China from 1979 to 1996 was around 56%. The shares of Taiwan, the United States, and Japan in cumulative utilized FDI in China by 1996 were 9%, 7.5%, and 7.9%, respectively.

Hong Kong's large share in China's investment conceals an important intermediary role for Hong Kong. In China's statistics, investment from Hong Kong includes the investment of the subsidiaries of foreign companies incorporated in Hong Kong. Many multinational companies like to test the Chinese investment environment through investments from their Hong Kong subsidiaries, because Hong Kong has the required expertise and is the foremost

Chapter 2

Table 2.4
Contracted Foreign Direct Investment in China by Source, 1979–96
(US$ million)

Year	Total	Investment Source			
		Hong Kong	Taiwan	United States	Japan
1979–85	16,325	10,799	n.a.	1,977	1,457
	(100)	(66.2)		(12.1)	(8.9)
1986	2,834	1,429	n.a.	527	210
	(100)	(50.4)		(18.6)	(7.4)
1987	3,709	1,947	85	342	301
	(100)	(52.5)	(2.3)	(9.2)	(8.1)
1988	5,297	3,467	359	370	276
	(100)	(65.5)	(6.8)	(7.0)	(5.2)
1989	5,600	3,160	427	641	439
	(100)	(56.4)	(7.6)	(11.4)	(7.8)
1990	6,596	3,833	943	358	457
	(100)	(58.1)	(14.3)	(5.4)	(6.9)
1991	11,977	7,215	1,341	548	812
	(100)	(60.2)	(11.2)	(4.6)	(6.8)
1992	58,124	40,044	5,543	3,121	2,173
	(100)	(68.9)	(9.5)	(5.4)	(3.7)
1993	111,436	73,939	9,965	6,813	2,960
	(100)	(66.4)	(8.9)	(6.1)	(2.7)
1994	82,680	46,971	5,395	6,010	4,440
	(100)	(56.8)	(6.5)	(7.3)	(5.4)
1995	91,282	40,996	5,849	7,471	7,592
	(100)	(44.9)	(6.4)	(8.2)	(8.3)
1979–95	395,860	233,800	29,907	28,178	21,117
	(100)	(59.1)	(7.6)	(7.1)	(5.3)
1996*	73,276	28,002	5,141	6,916	5,131
	(100)	(38.2)	(7.0)	(9.4)	(7.0)
1979–96	469,136	261,802	35,048	35,097	26,248
	(100)	(55.8)	(7.5)	(7.5)	(5.6)

Source: *Almanac of China's Foreign Relations and Trade*, various issues.
Note: * Preliminary data. Figures in brackets are row percentages.

Table 2.5
Utilized Foreign Direct Investment in China by Source, 1979–96
(US$ million)

| Year | | Investment Source | | | |
	Total	Hong Kong	Taiwan	United States	Japan
1979–85	4,721	3,134	n.a.	704	660
	(100)	(66.4)		(14.9)	(14.0)
1986	1,875	1,001	n.a.	315	201
	(100)	(53.4)		(16.8)	(10.7)
1987	2,314	1,588	53	263	220
	(100)	(68.6)	(2.3)	(11.4)	(9.5)
1988	3,194	2,068	217	236	515
	(100)	(64.7)	(6.8)	(7.4)	(16.1)
1989	3,393	2,037	258	284	356
	(100)	(60.0)	(7.6)	(8.4)	(10.5)
1990	3,487	1,880	499	456	503
	(100)	(53.9)	(14.3)	(13.1)	(14.4)
1991	4,366	2,405	489	323	533
	(100)	(55.1)	(11.2)	(7.4)	(12.2)
1992	11,008	7,507	1,051	511	710
	(100)	(68.2)	(9.5)	(4.6)	(6.4)
1993	27,515	17,275	3,139	2,063	1,324
	(100)	(62.8)	(11.4)	(7.5)	(4.8)
1994	33,767	19,665	3,391	2,491	2,075
	(100)	(58.2)	(10.0)	(7.4)	(6.1)
1995	37,521	20,060	3,162	3,083	3,108
	(100)	(53.5)	(8.4)	(8.2)	(8.3)
1979–95	133,161	78,620	12,259	9,710	10,205
	(100)	(59.0)	(9.2)	(7.3)	(7.7)
1996	41,726	20,677	3,475	3,443	3,679
	(100)	(49.6)	(8.3)	(8.3)	(8.8)
1979–96	174,887	99,297	15,734	13,153	13,884
	(100)	(56.8)	(9.0)	(7.5)	(7.9)

Source: *Almanac of China's Foreign Relation and Trade*, various issues.
Note: Figures in brackets are row percentages.

centre for China's trade and investment. Chinese enterprises also invest in China from their Hong Kong subsidiaries to take advantage of preferences given to foreign investors. There is no reliable estimate of the amount of Chinese capital "round tripping" via Hong Kong.

As Hong Kong is an international financial centre and there is a world capital market, it is not very meaningful to talk about the nationality of capital. Contrary to the predictions of Karl Marx, the proletariat of the world have not united, though the capitalists have. Whatever the true origin of Hong Kong capital, Hong Kong certainly plays a crucial mediation role in China-bound investment.

As expected, figures on contracted FDI were more volatile than utilized FDI. Contracted FDI from the United States dropped significantly in 1990 and 1991 following the Tiananmen incident, but contracted FDI from Hong Kong and Taiwan continued to rise. As Hong Kong and Taiwan together accounted for two-thirds of FDI in China, total contracted FDI in China continued to rise in 1990–91 despite the Tiananmen incident. Hong Kong investors responded rapidly to Deng Xiaoping's southern tour in support of economic reforms in early 1992. Hong Kong's share of China's contracted FDI jumped to 69% in 1992, and the shares of Taiwan, the United States, and Japan declined correspondingly. Since 1993 other countries have jumped on the bandwagon, and Hong Kong's share has gradually declined.

The difference in the reactions of Hong Kong and Taiwan investors and those of western investors are explained as follows. Investments from Hong Kong and Taiwan were more outward oriented, and they were affected more by conditions in the world market than the Chinese market. As conditions in the world market were stable in 1990 and 1991, investments from Taiwan and Hong Kong continued to rise. In contrast, the investments of the West were inward oriented, and they were affected more by the Chinese market, which went into a slump after the Tiananmen incident. Moreover, investors from Hong Kong and Taiwan had a better understanding of the Chinese situation. As early as 1990 they saw that China would continue with opening and economic reforms despite the Tiananmen incident, whereas western investors were still hesitant. Last, the investments of Hong Kong and Taiwan were concentrated in Guangdong and Fujian, which were comparatively stable during the Tiananmen incident.

Despite the rapid increase in FDI in China, investment from outside Greater China is still disproportionately small. By 1995 the stocks of utilized FDI of the United States and Japan in the Mainland were only roughly the same as their investments in Hong Kong. External investment in China came predominately from the CEA.

The "Chineseness" of FDI in China shows that China's investment environment is still inadequate by international standards. Investors from Taiwan and Hong Kong have been able to mitigate the inadequacy of legal protection through their kinship networks. However, it must be stressed that the Chinese investment environment is maturing. Hong Kong's share in China's contracted investment declined from a high of 69% in 1992 to 38% in 1996, and Hong Kong's share of China's utilized investment also declined from a high of 69% in 1992 to 45% in 1997.

Notes

1. Readers interested in a more detailed account can consult Sung 1991, chapters 1, 3, and 4.

2. Besides processing and assembling, other foreign investment also includes leasing and compensation trade. However, the latter two items are not important. Interested readers can consult Sung (1991, pp. 54–55).

3. From the mid-eighties till 1996, the investment in processing operations was greatly understated. However, the bias was rectified in 1997. Interested readers can consult Sung, Liu, Wong, and Lau (1995, pp. 63–68).

CHAPTER 3

Policy Changes and Economic Integration

Economic Integration

According to economic theory, economic integration means a lowering of the barriers to business between two economies. The barriers may be institutional (tariffs) or natural (transportation costs). In the jargon of economics, economic integration may not imply a tightly knit relationship. For instance, it has often been said that the decrease in the cost of transportation has led to global economic integration.

There are three different types of institutional barriers to international economic exchange:

1. Barriers to movement of goods, such as tariffs and quotas;
2. Barriers to movement of factors of production (labour and capital), such as controls on migration; or
3. Transaction costs and risks arising from the use of different currencies and such costs are significantly higher for countries that have strict foreign exchange controls.

There are also natural barriers such as geographic and cultural distance. Geographic and cultural affinities are often important in economic integration (e.g., emergence of the CEA). Empirically, it has been estimated that, other things being equal, sharing a common linguistic tie is associated with a big (more than 250%) increase in the bilateral FDI flow (Wei 1996, p. 1).

Many countries have entered into multilateral institutional agreements to promote economic integration. The most important among them is the GATT (General Agreement on Tariff and Trade), which was established after World War II to regulate international trade. At the Uruguay Round of trade negotiations, which concluded in December 1993, member countries decided to replace the GATT with the World Trade Organization (WTO) in 1995. The WTO oversees a comprehensive set of rules governing world commerce that cover not only trade in manufactured goods but also that in services and agricultural products as well as rules for intellectual property protection.

The two most important principles of the GATT are *liberalism* (minimal restrictions on international transactions) and *symmetry* (all nations should be treated in the same way). Each member must observe the Most Favoured Nations (MFN) clause, which stipulates that any tariff concessions made by a member to any other country must be extended to all members. This ensures the principle of symmetry and is central to the liberalization of world trade in the post-war era.

The formation of trade blocs usually violates the principle of symmetry, as members of the bloc receive favourable treatment that is not enjoyed by non-members. For instance, discriminatory tariff preferences (giving tariff preferences to some members but not others) violate the MFN clause and are usually not allowed by the GATT. However, the GATT allows the formation of Free Trade Areas (FTA) where free trade is practised among members.

Trade Blocs

The following different types of trade blocs, in ascending degree of economic integration, are usually distinguished:

1. Free trade area — member countries eliminate tariffs among themselves, and each member maintains its own tariff schedule on goods from outside countries.

2. Customs Union — Member countries eliminate tariffs among themselves and establish common tariff on outside goods. A customs union is a single bargaining entity in world trade.
3. Common Market — Customs union plus free factor movement.
4. Economic Union — Members integrate all economic policies.

The above forms of trade blocs are GATTable, as they are all based on the FTA. A major drawback of the FTA is the need to regulate internal trade despite abolition of internal tariffs. Otherwise, goods from nonmembers would enter the FTA through the member with the lowest tariffs, and individual members would not be able to maintain their own tariffs for outsiders. A customs union avoids the problem by having a common external tariff, but this means that individual members lose their autonomy in trade policies. All members must agree to a common policy and must also agree to the distribution of joint tariff revenues.

The North American Free Trade Area comprising Canada, Mexico, and the United States is the most prominent FTA. The European Economic Community (EEC) created by the 1957 Treaty of Rome is a common market trying to become an economic union. The EEC first changed its name to the European Community (EC) and then to the European Union (EU).

History of Economic Integration of the China Circle

Since the late 1980s the economies of the Mainland and Hong Kong have become highly integrated. Presently, the Mainland and Hong Kong are each other's foremost partners in investment and trade (if entrepôt trade via Hong Kong is included).

Despite the absence of official ties, economic integration has proceeded rapidly between the Mainland and Taiwan, largely through the use of the efficient intermediary services of Hong Kong. In 1991 Taiwan surpassed Hong Kong and the United States to become the second-largest supplier of goods (after Japan) to the Mainland and also surpassed the United States and Japan to become the second-largest investor (after Hong Kong) on the Mainland. In 1992 China surpassed Japan to become the second-largest market (after the United States) for Taiwan's exports.

Hong Kong and South China are much more tightly integrated than Taiwan and South China as a result of both geography and Taiwan's policy of no direct business links with China. There also is no land bridge connecting Taiwan with the Mainland. Unlike Taiwan, Hong Kong can fully exploit vertical complementarity by using trucks carrying semi-manufactured goods to its subsidiaries across the border. For Taiwan, investing in south China is not that different from investing in Southeast Asia in terms of labour costs, transportation costs, and turnaround time, although South China has the advantage of cultural proximity.

Though the economic relationships between Hong Kong and Guangdong, Taiwan and Fujian, and between Hong Kong and Taiwan are quite close, the economic ties between Guangdong and Fujian are not particularly strong. There is an absence of complementarity between the two provinces, as both lack natural resources and are at the same stage of economic development. The two are not highly rivalrous, either. They are links to separate communities of overseas Chinese with different dialects, thus moderating their competition for overseas investment.

Subregional Economic Integration

Greater South China or Greater Hong Kong was the first and most successful subregional economic zone in East Asia. As East Asian countries liberalized their economies in the 1980s, numerous subregional economic zones emerged as a result of geographic and market forces. Trade and investment flows grew among geographically contiguous but politically separate border areas, taking advantage of the complementarities in factor endowment and technological capacity among countries at different stages of economic development (Chia 1993). These subregional economic zones are variously called transnational export processing zones, natural economic territories (Scalapino 1992), and growth triangles (ASEAN terminology). They include the Tumen River area development project in Northeast Asia involving the Russian Far East, Mongolia, Northeast China, the Korean peninsula and Japan; the baht economic zone encompassing Thailand and the contiguous border areas of southwest China, Burma, Laos, Cambodia and Vietnam; the Mekong River Basin Project involving the riparian countries of Thailand, Burma, Vietnam, Laos, Cambodia, and southwest China; and three growth triangles of the ASEAN: the Southern Growth Triangle involving Singapore, the Johor state in Malaysia, and Batam island in Indonesia; the proposed Northern Growth Triangle encompassing Western Indonesia, northern Malaysia, and southern Thailand; and the proposed Eastern Growth Triangle involving Brunei, eastern Indonesia, the southern Philippines, and Sabah and Sarawak in eastern Malaysia (Chia 1993).

Integration via Cultural Affinity

Despite intense trade and investment flows among "the trio", there is an obvious lack of institutional integration. Because of Taiwan's ban on direct business deals with the Mainland, China and Taiwan are institutionally more closely integrated with most other economies than they are with each other.

Besides the lack of diplomatic and commercial ties, the three important institutional barriers to economic integration most often cited are tariffs, controls on factor movements, and exchange risks. On all three counts, barriers to economic integration among the trio are very high. For instance, take the case of the Mainland and Hong Kong. Even though Hong Kong became a Special Administrative Region of China in July 1997, it is specified in the Sino-British Agreement on Hong Kong that Hong Kong will remain a separate customs territory with its own currency. Migration from China to

Hong Kong will be strictly controlled. Even after 1997, Hong Kong and the Mainland will be less institutionally integrated than Greece and Ireland, both being members of the European Union, which have complete freedom of movement of goods and factors between them. Members of the European Monetary System within the European Union are even more closely integrated because of their pegged exchange rates. Since China is not a member of the WTO, and Chinese currency is not convertible. Hong Kong is institutionally more closely integrated with most other economies than with China.

Although economic theory concentrates on tariffs, controls on migration, and exchange integration, the effect of geographical and cultural distances may be even more important. Hong Kong is only a thirty-minute train ride from China, and Taiwan is also close to China. The importance of cultural affinity is quite evident. People in Hong Kong have their ancestral roots in Guangdong, the primary site of Hong Kong's investment in China. Taiwan also accounts for the bulk of investment in Fujian. These geographic and cultural proximities enable businesses to evade formal barriers to trade and investment. Tariffs can be evaded through smuggling, and there is rampant smuggling from Hong Kong and Taiwan to China. The movement of people from Hong Kong and Taiwan to China is relatively free, even though movement in the other direction is highly controlled. However, illegal immigrants from the Mainland are quite common in Hong Kong and Taiwan, as the labour markets in the two economies are extremely tight. Although the Chinese yuan is not convertible, Hong Kong currency circulates widely (and unofficially) in Guangdong, especially in the Shenzhen SEZ. The Hong Kong government estimates that 22% to 25% of the total supply of the Hong Kong currency (roughly HK$17 billion) circulates in China (*Hong Kong Economic Journal*, 5 May 1994). A grey market for yuan also existed in Hong Kong for some time. The grey market became an open market in 1994, when China officially permitted visitors to take 6,000 yuan out of or into China. Many Hong Kong tourists' shops now accept payment in yuan.

Cultural Affinity and Policy Change

Despite cultural and geographic affinity, the integration of the trio during the Cold War era was minimal. China's reform and opening is clearly necessary to the integration of the trio. However, policy change is by no means sufficient for economic integration. The world is littered with examples of failed agreements to enhance economic integration. The reform and opening of the former Soviet Union under Gorbachev did not lead to any significant increase in FDI or in exports. The Tumen River Project involving North Korea has not yet shown any significant results, despite support from the Asian Development Bank.

It should be stressed that policy formation does not take place in a vacuum. In China's case, the initial policies of opening and reform instituted in 1979 could have been reversed if the results had been poor. Thanks to cultural and geographic affinity, the opening of China led to rapid growth of FDI, exports, and GDP in Guangdong, and the results were evident in the mid-1980s. Guangdong's success has helped to strengthen the position of the reformers in Beijing and has enabled them to push for further reforms.

Reforms in China suffered a serious setback with the 1989 Tiananmen incident. The conservative leaders in Beijing have been able to neutralize the repeated calls for reforms and opening from Deng Xiaoping. In early 1992 Deng went to Guangdong, where reforms and opening were most successful, and he appealed to the nation to learn from Guangdong. He designated Guangdong as the "dragon head" of China's reform and opening. The role of the Hong Kong–Guangdong economic nexus in China's policy making is evident.

It should be stressed that, as a result of cultural and geographic proximity, the dynamism of the Hong Kong economy has been able to activate market forces in China, especially in Guangdong. The growth of market forces in Guangdong and China has pressed planners toward further reform and marketization. The best example of this is the growth of the black market in foreign exchange in China. The presence of an active black market forces planners to devalue the Renminbi and also to create a legal market for foreign exchange. The Hong Kong–Guangdong nexus also undercuts China's foreign trade monopoly. Many localities and enterprises have been able to trade with the outside world covertly through their Hong Kong connections, and China was forced to decentralize its foreign trade since then (Sung 1991, pp. 58–60).

Hong Kong–Mainland Relations in the Cold War Era

Before China's opening, economic ties linking the Mainland and Hong Kong were quite strong, but the relationship was asymmetric. Hong Kong was open to China's export and investment, and Hong Kong residents were able to visit their relatives in China, but reverse flows were largely barred. With the inauguration of China's economic reforms and open policy in 1978, the economic relationship between the Mainland and Hong Kong became more balanced and multifaceted. The details of these developments will be discussed later.

Before the Communist came to power in 1949, Hong Kong had been an important entrepôt for China. China could have taken Hong Kong by force in 1949, but Beijing chose to leave Hong Kong in British hands. This suggests that Beijing placed a high value on the role of Hong Kong as China's window to the outside world. Following China's entry into the Korean War in 1951, the United Nations embargoed sales of strategic materials to China, and the United States banned all imports from China. Strategic materials were smuggled from Hong Kong into China on a large scale, and the Hong Kong government did not crack down very hard on the illicit trade. Due to China's isolation, the value of Hong Kong as China's window to the world was enhanced.

Hong Kong's entrepôt trade nevertheless withered, partly as a result of the U.N. embargo and the U.S. ban, and partly because Beijing centralized international trade in the hands of the state and redirected China's trade to the Soviet bloc. The greater part of

China's trade in the 1950s was state-to-state trade handled directly by the government's foreign trade corporations, bypassing Hong Kong. China's imports from Hong Kong dwindled to negligible amounts. China's exports to Hong Kong continued to grow as a result of China's need to earn hard currency, particularly after the Sino-Soviet rift of the late 1950s.

With the withering of entrepôt trade, Hong Kong was deprived of its main means of livelihood. However, refugee capital and labour from China transformed Hong Kong into an industrial city and a dazzling example of success through an export-oriented strategy. Hong Kong became a lucrative market, and China's exports to Hong Kong grew rapidly in the 1960s and 1970s. In the 1960s Hong Kong was the Mainland's foremost market. China's trade surplus with Hong Kong was around one-fifth of its total exports, and China used the hard currency thus earned to finance imports of grain, industrial raw materials, and capital goods from developed countries. As China was isolated, it invested heavily in Hong Kong in order to use Hong Kong as a window to the world.

China's Policy Changes toward Hong Kong

In light of Hong Kong's long-standing position as China's window to the outside world, it is not surprising that China tailored its open-door policy to forge closer links with Hong Kong. The country allowed Guangdong to experiment with economic reforms and established SEZs to forge links with Hong Kong.

On paper, Hong Kong businesses receive no favourable concessions in China over other overseas businesses. In reality, however, due to geographical proximity and kinship links, Hong Kong businesses have a significant advantage. Hong Kong investors have been able to obtain favourable concessions from local authorities in Guangdong as a result of the kinship network. It is also easier for Hong Kong Chinese to visit the Mainland than it is for foreigners, as visas are not required for Hong Kong Chinese. China is thus more open to Hong Kong than to other economies.

It must be stressed that Hong Kong has played a pivotal role in China's opening, especially in the early years of the open policy. The development of Shenzhen, the most important SEZ, vividly illustrates the crucial role of Hong Kong in China's opening. In January 1979 the State Council created an industrial export zone at Shekou, which is close to Hong Kong. The zone was to be developed and managed by the China Merchants Company, a Hong Kong-based company controlled by the Chinese Ministry of Communications. According to Ho and Huenemann (1984, p. 49), "Hong Kong business interests suggested that the zone be expanded to encompass property development and tourism and suggested the name 'Special Economic Zone' to reflect the broader scope". Shekou thus became part of the Shenzhen SEZ. The 15% corporate tax rate of SEZs was designed to match the profit tax rate of Hong Kong, which had been 15%.

A number of Chinese officials, including Deng Xiaoping, consulted Hong Kong capitalists on the opening of Hainan. In June 1988 Deng remarked that China would build "a few Hong Kongs" on its soil, and that the situation in Hong Kong would remain unchanged even beyond the fifty years promised in the Sino-British declaration. Deng reiterated his wish to "build a few Hong Kongs" right after the suppression of the pro-democracy movement (*Ming Pao*, 29 June 1989), and Deng's support for the plan of the Yangpu free port in Hainan was cited as an example of such a policy.

In the early 1980s the elites in Hong Kong, including established British and local Hong Kong capital, were aware of the importance o f Hong Kong in China's opening. They reckoned that with successful long-run economic development China might become less dependent on Hong Kong. They thus seized the opportunity to open negotiations with China on settlement of the 1997 issue. They sought to extend the duration of British rule, perhaps at the cost of recognizing Chinese sovereignty in theory. China's response of "one country, two systems" was less than what the Hong Kong elites had expected, though they reluctantly accepted it because of the lack of a viable alternative. Nevertheless, China's willingness to sign an international treaty guaranteeing that capitalism remain in effect in Hong Kong for fifty years after 1997 must be recognized as unprecedented in the history of Chinese Communism. It shows that the Chinese leadership is well aware of the economic value of Hong Kong to China.

The Sino-British Declaration over the future of Hong Kong was signed in 1984. Chinese investment in Hong Kong increased sharply, as Hong Kong would be China's turf. The increasing involvement of China in the Hong Kong economy will be discussed in detail in Chapter 5.

Hong Kong's Policy Changes toward China

As Hong Kong is a free port, and the government generally follows non-interventionist economic policies, Hong Kong's policy changes toward China have not been dramatic. They have, however, been significant, especially in regard to restrictions against migrants from China.

As a free economy, Hong Kong is open to the whole world, including China. However, it should be noted that Hong Kong's controls on visitors from the Mainland are stricter than controls on visitors from other places. This is a result of the fear of illegal immigrants entering Hong Kong from the Mainland.

As is mentioned in Chapter 1, Hong Kong's abolition of the "touch base" policy in late 1980 led to a very tight labour market in Hong Kong. As a result, Hong Kong manufacturers have been relocating to Guangdong in droves since 1987.

Though the Hong Kong barrier against permanent migration from the Mainland is very strict, the barrier against temporary stays has relaxed in recent years. To deal with the labour shortage, the Hong Kong government embarked on a labour importation scheme in 1989. Since then many Chinese workers have come to Hong Kong to work on temporary contracts. The third labour importation scheme, announced in January 1992, doubled the labour intake quota to 25,000 workers, practically all of which are from China. However, the quota was slashed to 1,000 in 1995 because of rising unemployment in Hong Kong.

The barriers against the entry of professionals from China have also been relaxed, and such professionals are now eligible to become permanent residents of Hong Kong. Since 1990 Hong Kong employers have been permitted to employ mainland professionals who have remained overseas for over two years. In April 1994 the Hong Kong government announced a trial scheme to import 1,000 mainland graduates.

It should be noted that there are few restrictions against mainlanders entering Hong Kong on official passports, and it is estimated that by March 1994 65,600 mainland cadres were working in mainland companies in Hong Kong (Lin and Kan 1996, p. 131). Because of the tight labour market in Hong Kong, there is also a substantial but unknown number of illegal immigrants as well as of short-term visitors from the Mainland participating illegally in the labour market. In the space of a few years, tourists from the Mainland have increased from a trickle to 2.24 million in 1995, accounting for 22% of total tourist arrivals in Hong Kong. China surpassed Taiwan as the foremost source of tourists to Hong Kong from 1994 to 1995. However, Japan surpassed the Mainland as the foremost source of tourists to Hong Kong in 1996.

The Hong Kong government also relaxed the restrictions against civil servants travelling to China and Taiwan in the 1980s. Such restrictions were a legacy of the Cold War. All the aforementioned changes have promoted the reintegration of Hong Kong and China.

Mainland–Taiwan Relations

During the Cold War era, Mainland–Taiwan economic exchanges were all but non-existent. Taiwan, however, purchased herbal medicine from the Mainland indirectly via Hong Kong through officially approved importers. The herbs could not be grown on Taiwan.

With the inauguration of economic reforms and the open-door policy in China in December 1978, Beijing called for the establishment of "three links (mail, travel, and trade) and four exchanges (science, culture, sports, and arts)" with Taiwan on New Year's Day, 1979. On the same day, the United States established diplomatic relations with the Mainland and broke off its long-standing diplomatic relations with Taiwan. Faced with diplomatic isolation, Taiwan nevertheless adhered to its original schedule of liberalization and lifted its ban on overseas travel for tourist purposes on the same day. Though Taiwan responded to Beijing's overture with a reaffirmation of the old "three no's policy" of no contact, no negotiations, and no compromise, Taiwan's relaxation of tourist travel constituted a "known loophole" in the policy of no contact. Taiwanese can meet their mainland relatives in third countries or can even secretly visit them on the Mainland by going through Hong Kong or other places. Before November 1987, when the ban on travel to the Mainland was lifted, around 10,000 Taiwanese secretly visited the Mainland every year (Wakabayashi, 1990, p. 6).

Beijing took additional steps to promote exchanges with Taiwan in 1980, including sending a delegation to Hong Kong to buy US$80 million worth of Taiwanese goods, and the value of the Mainland's imports from Taiwan in 1980 jumped to 11.5 times the 1979 figure. China also abolished the tariff on Taiwanese goods in 1980 on the grounds that Taiwan is a part of China, and import approvals for Taiwanese goods were given priority over other goods. China's import of Taiwanese goods rose so rapidly that Taiwan had insufficient stocks, and China imported many defective products. China also imported a lot of Hong Kong goods with fake Taiwanese documents. To rectify the chaos, Beijing levied "adjustment taxes" on Taiwanese goods in May 1981, though Taiwanese goods still had an advantage, as the adjustment taxes were slightly lower than tariffs were.

On 30 September 1981, Ye Jianying, Chairman of the Standing Committee of the National People's Congress, announced the famous "Nine-Point Proposal" calling for peaceful reunification through negotiation, allowing Taiwan to maintain its capitalist system and army. Taiwan would enjoy a high degree of autonomy as a "special administrative region (SAR)" of China. In January 1982 Deng Xiaoping announced that the "one country, two systems" formula would apply to Taiwan as well as to Hong Kong.

Taiwan gradually softened its interpretation of the "three no's policy" to cope with the reality of increasing contacts and thriving indirect trade. In July 1985 it indicated that it would not interfere in indirect exports, as it could not control them. Indirect imports, however, would still be subject to control. Import controls on mainland products have gradually been liberalized beginning in 1987. The number of items Taiwan allowed to be indirectly imported increased from 29 items (July 1987) to 90 items (January 1989) to 155 items (early 1990) and then to 1,654 items by the end of 1993 (Yeh 1995, p. 62). In July 1996 Taiwan liberalized by changing from positive licensing to negative licensing, i.e., imports will be freely allowed unless they fall within the controlled list. Positive licensing was retained for agricultural products, however.

Taiwan's Policy Changes and Interactions with the Mainland

Taiwan's export-oriented growth since 1960 has been very success-ful. Like Hong Kong, Taiwan has accumulated valuable human capital for the export of labour-intensive products. This knowledge has increasing returns and has fed an explosive growth process, leading to persistent trade surpluses in the 1970s. These surpluses exploded in the early 1980s with the appreciation of the U.S. dollar under President Ronald Reagan. Taiwan's current account surplus reached 20% of the GNP in 1986 (Naughton 1997, pp. 86–87).

To cope with this huge disequilibrium, Taiwan should have revalued its currency and relaxed its foreign exchange controls to promote outward foreign investment. However, the government was wary of hurting the interests of export-dependent manufactur-ers and refused to revalue. It delayed adjustment by building up huge foreign exchange reserves that represented "foreign invest-ment" by the government. This led to the diversion of resources into low-yielding assets and also generated trade fractions with the United States. Moreover, Taiwan's domestic investment declined, as investors were expecting a revaluation, which implies cheaper imported equipment. The situation became more and more untenable (Naughton, 1997, pp. 88–89).

The United States, as well as the logic of the situation, finally forced a revaluation in 1986. Taiwan's currency was revalued by 40% against the U.S. dollar in two years. Foreign exchange controls were relaxed in July 1987, partly in response to U.S. pressure, and indirect investment on the Mainland increased rapidly.

In November 1987 Taiwan lifted the ban on visiting relatives on the Mainland. In October 1989 it promulgated regulations sanctioning indirect trade, investment, and technical co-operation with China.

The Mainland's opening eased the adjustment process for Taiwan. Were it not for the opportunity to invest in the Mainland, revaluation would have implied the obsolescence of Taiwan's human capital in the production and export of labour-intensive products.

It happens that Taiwan's liberalization and *rapprochement* with the Mainland coincided with the third wave of the opening of China in 1987–88 under the slogan of the "Coastal Development Strategy". Before 1987 China tried to attract high-tech investment and also tried to increase domestic content and backward linkages. Labour-intensive and low-tech investment was not welcome except in Guangdong, where provincial policies have been more pragmatic than they have been elsewhere in China. This implies that the pace of foreign investment in China (except in Guangdong) was not very fast. The Coastal Development Strategy was launched by Zhao Ziyang, and the strategy accepts low-tech, labour-intensive processing operations geared for exports. Preferential policies for foreign investors were strengthened. Fully foreign-owned ventures, which were severely restricted before 1987, became much more common. This is important for Taiwanese investors who have a preference for fully foreign-owned ventures (Naughton 1997, pp. 91–92).

A 1988 State Council decree gave Taiwanese investors favourable treatment over other foreign investors (Sung 1992, p. 8). Local authorities also tend to give Taiwanese investors more favourable treatment in terms of a faster approval process or better supporting services.

China is planning to abolish the special favours for Taiwanese and overseas Chinese investors as part of the reform package to gain entry into the WTO. However, Hong Kong residents and Taiwanese will continue to enjoy simpler border formalities and probably special informal treatment from local authorities in Guangdong and Fujian.

Taiwan's Reinterpretation of Its "Three No's" Policy

Though the Mainland is more open to Taiwan than to any other economy, Taiwan is less open to the Mainland than to other economy. Taiwan still bans direct business links with China, though what constitutes "direct links" has been gradually softened and reinterpreted.

On 23 February 1991 Taiwan promulgated a policy on national reunification. Taiwan would abandon its policy of "three no's" and would establish official contact with the Mainland on the condition that the Mainland soften its drive to isolate Taiwan diplomatically and abandon its threat of using force against Taiwan. If these friendly gestures were not extended, Taiwan would continue to shun official contact with the Mainland. However, Taiwan would gradually develop its unofficial exchanges with the Mainland. Bilateral issues would be dealt with by the Straits Exchange Foundation, a semi-official body established by Taipei.

On 1 May 1991 Taiwan officially terminated the "Period of Communist Rebellion" on the Mainland, declaring an end to the four decades of civil war across the Taiwan Straits. This enabled Taiwan to adopt a more pragmatic policy towards the Mainland. At the same time, a delegation from the Straits Foundation visited

Beijing for the first time and requested co-operation in solving problems such as privacy in the Taiwan Straits and illegal immigrants entering Taiwan from the Mainland. Beijing responded to Taiwan's moves, and a channel of dialogue was established in April 1993 between the Taiwan Straits Foundation and China's Association of the Taiwan Straits.

It should be noted that Taiwan has gradually liberalized the interpretation of "indirect links", partly as a result of the ingenuity of Taiwanese businesspeople who circumvent Taiwan's ban by switching trade documents. Taiwanese exporters claim that their goods are destined for Hong Kong when the goods leave Taiwan. However, on arrival in Hong Kong, the trade documents are switched, and the new documents claim that the goods are destined for the Mainland. As the goods are consigned to a buyer in the Mainland, they do not go through Hong Kong customs, and no Hong Kong firm claims legal possession of them. Such goods are regarded as transshipment or "cargo in transit" by the Hong Kong government and are not regarded as part of Hong Kong's trade. Such trade is called "direct trade" in this paper, because it looks like indirect trade in terms of trade documentation, as it involves two separate sets of trade documents, but it is direct trade in reality because no third party buys the goods involved for resale. By switching trade documents, Taiwanese exporters save the cost of going through Hong Kong customs. Since the early 1990s Taiwan has accepted "switch bills" as indirect trade, partly because the government is quite powerless to stop the trade.

Taiwan has also liberalized the interpretation of indirect investment. Small investors do not have to form subsidiaries overseas. Starting in 1992, for investment under US$1 million, the investor has been able to remit the funds to China as long as this is done through a third place.

Since the opening of the Macau International Airport in 1996, Taiwanese have been able to fly to the Mainland without changing planes, though the plane has to touch down in Macau and also change its flight number for the second leg of the journey.

Tension and Rapprochement across the Taiwan Straits

China's military exercises in the Taiwan Straits in late 1995 and early 1996 reminded the world that the continual economic integration of the China Circle is not a forgone conclusion. However, the episode did demonstrate that China's naval power is not yet strong enough to carry out an invasion. After the successful re-election of Lee Teng Hui to Presidency in Taiwan, Beijing conducted a high-level meeting on the Taiwan issue in May 1996. China decided to be firm on political matters. However, on economic issues, the Mainland would try to increase links with Taiwan. Beijing thus resumed its policy of wooing Taiwanese businessmen. However, Taiwan's plan to develop Taipei as a regional operations centre has suffered a serious setback, as investors are nervous about the possible outbreak of hostilities in the future.

Taiwan has not returned Beijing's recent friendly gestures. On 15 August 1996 Lee Teng Hui announced that restrictions should be placed on Taiwanese companies investments in the Mainland (*Hong Kong Economic Journal*, 16 August 1996). Though the precise nature of the restrictions have not been announced, Taiwanese businesspeople have reacted unfavourably to the announcement. Formosa Plastics called off a US$3 billion power plant project in China, and food giant President Enterprises halted its US$100 million project to set up a power plant in the central city of Wuhan.

On 22 January 1997 Taiwan and China concluded an agreement in Hong Kong to allow ships owned by Taiwanese or mainlanders that carry flags of convenience to sail direct between Kaohsiung and two mainland ports in Fujian, Xiamen, and Fuzhou. This is a far cry from full-scale direct shipping, as Taiwan only allows the ships to carry cargo between the Mainland and third countries via a transshipment zone in Kaohsiung. Direct shipping of Taiwanese cargo to the Mainland and vice versa are not allowed. As the transshipment zone is outside Taiwanese customs, it is not considered to be a violation of Taiwan's prohibition on direct shipping.

The impact on Hong Kong is estimated to be less than 1% of Hong Kong's shipping. However, the impact on Hong Kong of a full-scale direct shipping development could be more serious, as cross-Straits transshipment via Hong Kong amounted to one million containers in 1995, or 8% of Hong Kong's container throughput (*The Hong Kong Standard*, 23 January 1997). Moreover, shipping traffic from China to the United States could stop in Taiwan rather than in Hong Kong, and Hong Kong is currently the transshipment centre for 80% of all United States-bound mainland cargo.

Despite the clamour from Taiwan's business community to allow direct links with the Mainland, the Taiwanese government is moving very slowly. This is because the Taiwanese government perceives that direct links with the Mainland are one of its few bargaining chips in future negotiations with the Mainland.

Hong Kong–Taiwan Relations

During the Cold War era, Hong Kong had no official ties with Taiwan, as Britain recognized Beijing in 1949 and broke off its diplomatic ties with Taiwan. Hong Kong banned Taiwan officials from entering Hong Kong on official business in 1955, after Taiwan agents sabotaged an aeroplane carrying mainland diplomats from Hong Kong to Jarkata for the Bandung Conference.

Despite the Hong Kong ban on Taiwan officials, trade between Hong Kong and Taiwan increased rapidly as both economies achieved very high growth rates. However, before 1987, the economic ties between Hong Kong and Taiwan were one-sided because of Taiwan's trade protectionism and foreign exchange controls. However, economic ties between Hong Kong and Taiwan developed extremely rapidly in the late 1980s with the liberalization of Taiwan's imports and foreign exchange controls, the sharp appreciation of the Taiwanese currency, and Taiwan's use of Hong Kong as an intermediary in its interactions with the Mainland. In April 1991 Taiwan established the Taipei Centre in Hong Kong to help Taiwanese investors establish paper companies in Hong Kong for investment in the Mainland. Hua Nan Commercial Bank, one of the

three largest commercial banks in Taiwan, was the first Taiwanese
bank to receive permission to operate a branch in Hong Kong in
July 1993 (*South China Morning Post*, 19 July 1993).

With the rapid growth in economic links and the lessening of
tension across the Taiwan Strait, official or semi-official relations
between Hong Kong and Taiwan have improved despite the
absence of diplomatic ties. The Hong Kong Trade Development
Council opened an office in Taipei in 1988 to promote Hong Kong
exports. In 1991 the Hong Kong government allowed a Taiwan
official, John Ni, to come to Hong Kong to head the Zhonghua
Travel Service, which was the covert Taiwan representation in
Hong Kong. The action broke the 1955 ban on Taiwan officials
entering Hong Kong on official business.

Taiwan continues to rely on Hong Kong as its middleman after
1997 because re-routing Taiwan's trade and investment with the
Mainland through other places could be much more costly. Taiwan's plan distinguishes Hong Kong as a special region from the
Mainland as long as Hong Kong remains a "free and democratic
economic entity" (*United Daily News*, 8 May 1993), and Taiwan's
air and shipping links with Hong Kong are treated as special links
that are neither domestic nor international. Taiwan's plans, however, must receive Beijing's blessing, because the Sino-British
Declaration specifies that Hong Kong's air and shipping links with
Taiwan have to be approved by Beijing. In late May 1997 Hong
Kong and Taiwan reached an agreement on shipping. Taiwanese
vessels are allowed to enter Hong Kong without hoisting a flag. It
appears that Beijing, partly out of concern for Hong Kong's economic interests, is allowing Taiwan to use Hong Kong as a
middleman after 1997.

CHAPTER 4

Trade between Hong Kong and the Mainland

Hong Kong and the Mainland are often considered each other's foremost trading partners. This assumption is misleading because it includes Mainland's trade with third countries via Hong Kong (Hong Kong's entrepôt trade). As is mentioned in Chapter 1, this book relies on Hong Kong's re-export statistics to estimate Mainland's trade with Hong Kong and Taiwan.

Hong Kong's Re-export Statistics and the Re-export Margin

The re-export margin is the difference in value between re-exports and imports for re-exports. It includes costs of storage, transportation within Hong Kong, and may be costs of packaging and minor processing that are not sufficiently substantial to change the form and nature of the product (otherwise, the products will be regarded as Hong Kong's *domestic exports*, i.e. exports made in Hong Kong, and not as *re-exports*).

Though the Hong Kong government has detailed statistics on imports, domestic exports, and re-exports, there are no statistics on imports for re-exports, because the importer may not be able to ascertain whether the imported good will be re-exported or not. A good imported into Hong Kong may change hands many times before eventual re-exportation. The re-export margin can thus only be obtained through survey data. Given the re-export margin, imports for re-export can be obtained from the value of re-exports.

Table 4.1
Hong Kong's Re-exports Margin by Origin, 1989–96

Year	Mainland	Others	Overall
1989	13.0%	11.5%	12.2%
1990	21.1%	12.7%	17.4%
1991	25.8%	10.3%	18.9%
1992	29.7%	10.3%	20.8%
1993	35.3%	8.5%	22.4%
1994	33.2%	6.0%	20.0%
1995	32.8%	5.9%	19.8%
1996	34.4%	6.6%	21.4%

Source: *Hong Kong Monthly Digest of Statistics*, Census and Statistics Department, Hong Kong, May 1997.

Then the value of retained imports (i.e., imports retained in Hong Kong for internal use) is obtained as the difference between total imports and imports for re-exports.

The Census and Statistics Department of the Hong Kong government has conducted surveys on Hong Kong's re-export margin, and the results were first released in February 1996 (Census and Statistics Department, 1996a). The rate of re-export margin for Chinese goods rose from 13% in 1989 to a record 35.3% in 1993 and then declined (Table 4.1). The increase in the rate is largely a result of the rise in the share of products from outward-processing operations in Hong Kong's re-exports of Chinese origin. In this book, the rate of re-export margin before 1989 is assumed to be the same as that of 1989 (13%) and the rate of re-export margin in 1997 is assumed to be the same as that in 1996.

Besides the re-export margin, we should also take into account the cost of insurance and freight. For the case of Hong Kong's re-exports of mainland goods to North America, this is 1% between the Mainland and Hong Kong, and 4.3% between Hong Kong and North America.

In 1996, for Chinese goods re-exported via Hong Kong, the North America c.i.f. price was thus 42% higher than China's f.o.b. price ($1.01 \times 1.344 \times 1.043 = 1.42$). For Chinese goods re-exported via Hong Kong, the c.i.f. – f.o.b. differential is huge. Ignoring this differential will result in bad estimates.

Hong Kong's Commodity Trade with the Mainland

Given the re-export margins, we can estimate the figures in Tables 4.2a and 4.2b, which include the value of Hong Kong's retained imports from the Mainland and that of those re-exported elsewhere, and the value of Hong Kong's domestic exports and re-exports to the Mainland. In this section, Mainland's exports to (imports from) Hong Kong are taken to be Hong Kong's imports from (exports to) the Mainland because the c.i.f. – f.o.b. differential of Hong Kong–Mainland trade is only 1%.

Hong Kong was the largest market for Chinese products in the late 1960s and early 1970s, consuming around 16% of China's exports. Another 4% of China's exports were re-exported via Hong Kong to third countries. Hong Kong thus accounted for around 20% of China's exports in total. Food was the major item of trade, accounting for over half of China's export consumed in Hong Kong. As China's imports from Hong Kong were negligible, China's trade surplus with Hong Kong was around one-fifth of China's total exports, and China used the hard currency thus earned to finance its imports of grain, industrial raw materials, and capital goods from developed countries.

China–Hong Kong trade was transformed in the post-reform period, however, with the re-exported portion of China's exports to Hong Kong growing rapidly, to the point that they exceeded the retained portion by 1985. China's imports of Hong Kong goods and also of Hong Kong re-exports increased rapidly. Hong Kong re-emerged as a major entrepôt for China, and China also became a major market for Hong Kong products.

Outward-Processing Trade

One reason for the rapid increase in trade between Hong Kong and China in the reform era is that Hong Kong's investments in outward

Chapter 4

Table 4.2a
Hong Kong–Mainland Trade, 1950–97
(US$ million)

	Hong Kong's Imports from Mainland			Hong Kong's Exports to Mainland		
	Total	Retained in Hong Kong	Re-exported Elsewhere	Total	Hong Kong Goods	Hong Kong Re-exports
1931–38	87	16	70	88	9	79
1950	137	–	–	221	–	–
1951	151	–	–	281	–	–
1952	145	–	–	91	–	–
1955	157	–	–	32	–	–
1960	207	–	–	21	2	19
1965	487	384	103	12	3	10
1970	468	362	106	11	5	6
1975	1,378	1,047	331	33	6	28
1977	1,734	1,233	501	44	7	38
1979	3,045	2,043	1002	383	121	263
1981	5,315	3,163	2,152	1,961	523	1,438
1983	5,891	3,352	2,539	2,531	856	1,676
1985	7,449	3,515	3,934	7,857	1,950	5,907
1987	14,775	5,213	9,562	11,290	3,574	7,669
1989	24,432	3,077	21,355	18,816	5,548	13,268
1990	29,528	4,019	25,509	20,305	6,086	14,219
1991	36,711	4,427	32,284	26,631	6,976	19,656
1992	44,187	3,967	40,220	35,136	7,943	27,193
1993	50,165	4,610	45,555	43,683	8,191	35,491
1994	58,702	5,655	53,047	49,670	7,895	41,776
1995	67,300	5,492	61,808	57,904	8,222	49,682
1996	71,148	4,798	66,350	61,982	7,967	54,015
1997	75,194	5,670	69,524	65,583	8,249	57,334

Sources: Hong Kong data — 1931–38: Tom C. F. (1957), *Entrepôt Trade and the Monetary Standards of Hong Kong*, Chicago, University of Chicago Press; 1948 and after: *Hong Kong Trade Statistics*; 1966 and after: *Review of Overseas Trade*, Census and Statistics Department, Hong Kong.

Chinese data — 1931–48: U.N. Statistical Office, *Yearbook of International Trade Statistics*; 1950–79: *China Statistical Yearbook*, China Statistical Publishing House, Beijing; 1981 and after: *China Customs Statistics*, Economic Information and Agency, Hong Kong.

Table 4.2b
Hong Kong–Mainland Trade, 1950–97
(%)

	Hong Kong's Imports from Mainland as percentage of Mainland's exports			Hong Kong's Exports to Mainland as percentage of Mainland's imports		
	Total	Retained in Hong Kong	Re-exported Elsewhere	Total	Hong Kong Goods	Re-exports
1931–38	31	5.8	25.2	21.5	2.2	19.3
1950	24.8			37.9		
1951	20.0			23.5		
1952	17.6			8.1		
1955	11.1			1.9		
1960	11.2			1.1	0.1	1.0
1965	21.8	17.2	4.6	0.7	0.2	0.5
1970	20.7	16.0	4.7	0.5	0.2	0.3
1975	19.0	14.4	4.6	0.5	0.1	0.4
1977	22.9	16.3	6.6	0.6	0.1	0.5
1979	22.3	15.0	7.3	2.5	0.8	1.7
1981	24.2	14.4	9.8	8.9	2.4	6.5
1983	26.5	15.1	11.4	11.8	4.0	7.8
1985	27.3	12.9	14.4	18.6	4.6	14.0
1987	37.5	13.2	24.3	26.1	8.3	17.8
1989	46.6	5.9	40.7	31.8	9.4	22.4
1990	47.6	6.5	41.1	38.1	11.4	26.7
1991	51.1	6.2	44.9	41.7	10.9	30.8
1992	52.0	4.7	47.3	45.1	10.2	34.9
1993	54.7	5.0	49.7	42.0	7.9	34.1
1994	48.6	4.7	43.9	42.9	6.8	36.1
1995	45.3	3.7	41.6	43.8	6.2	37.6
1996	47.1	3.2	43.9	44.6	5.7	38.9
1997	41.1	3.1	38.0	46.1	5.8	40.3

Sources: See Table 4.2a.

processing in China have generated huge trade flows. In outward processing, the mainland partners of Hong Kong firms (which can be processing operations or foreign-invested enterprises) process raw materials and semi-manufactured goods produced in Hong Kong or purchased by the Hong Kong parent in the world market, and the processed output is sold via the parent to the world market. Outward processing thus increases both the domestic exports of semi-manufactured goods from Hong Kong to China and also Hong Kong's China-related entrepôt trade.

Table 4.3 shows Hong Kong's trade involving outward processing in China. In 1997 Hong Kong's imports from China involving outward processing amounted to US $63.4 billion, or 81% of Hong Kong's total imports from China. The bulk of Hong Kong's imports involving outward processing were re-exported to third countries. These imports may have been further processed or packaged in Hong Kong before re-exportation. Since 1991 Hong Kong's re-exports of China origin involving outward processing exceeded Hong Kong's domestic exports. By 1997 the value of Hong Kong's re-exports of China origin involving outward processing was US$76.9 billion, or 2.8 times the amount of Hong Kong's domestic exports.

Over 70% of Hong Kong's domestic exports to China is related to outward processing. The share of re-exports to China related to outward processing declined from 50.3% in 1990 to 43.2% in 1996. This is a result of China's import liberalization. However, for both imports from China and re-exports of China origin, the proportions related to outward processing are high and rising. In 1997 outward processing accounted for 81% of Hong Kong's imports from China and 88% of Hong Kong's re-exports of China origin.

China's Trade with Hong Kong Itself and with Others via Hong Kong

With China's opening, Hong Kong regained its historic role as China's entrepôt. China's trade with other economies via Hong

Trade between Hong Kong and the Mainland 73

Table 4.3
Hong Kong's Trade Involving Outward Processing in the Mainland, 1989–97
(US$ million)

	Trade Involving Outward Processing in China						
	Exports to China			Imports from		Re-exports of China Origin	Hong Kong Domestic Exports
	Domestic Exports	Re-exports	Total	China	Guang-dong		
1989	4,098	5,757	9,855	14,562	13,601	—	28,731
(i)	(76.0)	(43.6)	(53.0)	(58.1)	—	—	—
1990	4,676	7,125	11,800	18,629	17,592	—	28,999
(i)	(79.0)	(50.3)	(58.8)	(61.8)	—	—	—
(ii)	(14.1)	(23.8)	(19.7)	(27.9)	(29.3)	—	(0.9)
1991	5,195	9,466	14,661	25,400	24,011	28,497	29,732
(i)	(76.5)	(48.2)	(55.5)	(67.6)	—	(74.1)	—
(ii)	(11.1)	(32.9)	(24.3)	(36.4)	(36.5)	—	(2.5)
1992	5,719	12,578	18,297	32,566	30,335	38,733	30,245
(i)	(74.3)	(46.2)	(52.4)	(72.1)	—	(78.3)	—
(ii)	(10.1)	(32.9)	(24.8)	(28.2)	(26.3)	(35.9)	(1.7)
1993	5,835	14,870	20,706	38,160	35,617	47,122	28,815
(i)	(74.0)	(42.1)	(47.9)	(73.8)	—	(80.8)	—
(ii)	(2.0)	(18.2)	(13.1)	(17.2)	(17.4)	(21.7)	(–4.7)
1994	5,429	18,015	23,444	45,925	43,372	54,677	28,739
(i)	(71.4)	(43.3)	(47.7)	(75.9)	—	(82.0)	—
(ii)	(–7.0)	(17.0)	(13.2)	(20.4)	(21.8)	(16.0)	(–0.3)
1995	5,673	22,456	28,130	51,650	49,068	63,658	29,945
(i)	(71.4)	(45.4)	(74.4)	(74.4)	—	(82.2)	—
(ii)	(4.5)	(24.7	(20.0)	(12.5)	(13.1)	(16.4)	(4.2)
1996	5,571	23,175	28,746	58,558	55,698	71,479	27,432
(i)	(72.8)	(43.2)	(46.9)	(79.9)	—	(86.0)	—
(ii)	(–1.8)	(3.2)	(2.2)	(13.4)	(13.5)	(12.3)	(–8.4)
1997	6,081	25,550	31,630	63,439	59,890	76,920	27,307
(i)	(76.1)	(44.7)	(48.6)	(81.2)	—	(88.4)	—
(ii)	(9.2)	(10.2)	(10.0)	(8.3)	(7.5)	(7.6)	(–0.5)

Source: *Hong Kong External Trade*, Census and Statistics Department, Hong Kong, various issues.

Notes: (i) Proportion of outward-processing trade in total (%).
(ii) Growth rate (%) over previous year.

Kong has increased much faster than China's trade with Hong Kong itself. From 1979 to 1997 China's trade with Hong Kong itself rose absolutely from US$2.2 billion to US$13.9 billion. However, as a share of China's trade, it declined from 7.4% to 4.3%. China's trade via Hong Kong with third countries increased much faster, rising a hundredfold — from US$1.3 billion (4.3% of China's trade) to US$127 billion (39%) of China's trade. The share of China exports re-exported via Hong Kong rose from 7.3% in 1979 to a peak of 49.7% in 1993, and then declined to 38% in 1997 (Table 4.2). The share of China imports re-exported from Hong Kong to China rose from 1.7% in 1979 to 40.3% in 1997. As the determinants of entrepôt trade and China's trade with Hong Kong itself are quite different, they are treated separately below.

China's Trade with Hong Kong Itself: Exports

Since 1979 China's exports via Hong Kong to other countries have increased tremendously, but China's exports retained for internal use in Hong Kong have stagnated since the late 1980s. Hong Kong was the largest final market (i.e., excluding Chinese exports via Hong Kong) for Chinese exports in the late 1960s and early 1970s. However, the Hong Kong market was overtaken by the Japanese market and the U.S. market in 1973 and 1987, respectively. In 1997, though Hong Kong accounted for 41.1% of China's exports, the bulk of these were re-exported, and the part retained in Hong Kong only represented 3.1% of China's exports.

The value of Hong Kong's imports of Chinese goods in 1997 totalled US$75.2 billion. Ninety-three per cent of these imports were re-exported to other countries, and only 7% were retained in Hong Kong. Although China was by far the foremost supplier of Hong Kong's re-exports, it only supplied 7.6% of Hong Kong's retained imports in 1997, ranking fourth after Japan, the United States, and Taiwan.

China has been unable to capture the higher end of Hong Kong's market dominated by Japan. Given the increasing affluence of Hong Kong and the Japanese dominance in vehicles, capital goods, and quality consumer durables and consumer goods, the future of Chinese products in Hong Kong is not very bright.

China's Trade with Hong Kong Itself: Imports

As Hong Kong's re-exports withered in the Cold War era, the bulk of its exports were domestic exports (exports of goods made in Hong Kong), and the United States had been the foremost market for Hong Kong's domestic exports from 1959 to 1992. China's imports from Hong Kong were negligible.

With China's opening, China's imports of Hong Kong goods soared. These were mostly semi-manufactured goods made and supplied by Hong Kong firms for their subsidiaries in the Mainland. By 1984 Hong Kong became the third-largest supplier of goods to China, after Japan and the United States. The share of Hong Kong goods in China's imports rose from an insignificant 0.8% in 1979 to a record 11.4% in 1990. Hong Kong was then China's third-largest supplier, after Japan (14.2%) and the United States (12.3%). However, with the liberalization of China's trade and the jump in Taiwanese investment, Taiwan surpassed Hong Kong and the United States in 1991 to become the second-largest supplier, with Hong Kong slipping to fourth place. In 1997 the share of Hong Kong goods in Chinese imports slipped to 5.8%.

As a result of the rapid growth of China's imports of Hong Kong goods, China became the foremost market for Hong Kong goods in 1993, taking 28% of Hong Kong's domestic exports, surpassing the United States, which had a 27% share. Though China's share slipped behind that of the United States temporarily in 1994, China emerged again as the foremost market in 1995. In 1997 it took 30.2% of Hong Kong's domestic exports, and the U.S. share declined to 26.1%.

China's Trade with Third Economies via Hong Kong

Hong Kong's China-related entrepôt trade has increased extremely rapidly in the reform era. Around 35% of this entrepôt trade has been traditional or pure entrepôt trade for which the Hong Kong trader acts as a middleman, and the rest (65%) has been related to Hong Kong's outward-processing activities in China. Both types of entrepôt trade have become prominent since 1979.

The rapid growth of entrepôt trade related to outward processing can easily be explained, as it is related to the relocation of Hong Kong manufacturing to China. The rapid increase in China-related traditional entrepôt trade is more difficult to explain, as China has established numerous direct links, including diplomatic, commercial, and transportation ties, with the rest of the world since the inauguration of its open policy. Paradoxically, the middleman role of Hong Kong is becoming more prominent, and an increasing share of China's commodity trade that is not related to outward processing is being handled through Hong Kong. To explain this paradox, it is worth constructing a theory of intermediation. The theory has strong predictions for entrepôt and services trade.

Theory of the Middleman

Since its adoption of an open-door policy in 1979, it has been easier to trade directly with China. The transaction costs of establishing a direct trade link have gone down, and this should lead to a rise in direct relative to indirect trade. However, China started to decentralize its foreign trade system in 1979, replacing vertical channels of command with horizontal links. The number of trading partners and trade links multiplied rapidly, creating a huge demand for intermediation. Before 1979, establishing trade links with ten state Trading Corporations would have ensured complete coverage of China trade. The number of trading corporations increased to over 1000 by 1984. It has become very costly for an individual firm to establish trade links with the mushrooming number of Chinese trading corporations. Intermediation emerged to economize on the cost of establishing trade links, and this demand for intermediation was channelled to Hong Kong because of its comparative advantage in trading. China's foreign trade decentralization came in three waves: one in 1979, one in 1984, and one in 1988. The share of

China's trade through Hong Kong jumped after each wave of decentralization.

The market composition of China's indirect trade via Hong Kong and the change over time of these markets in dependency on Hong Kong's entrepôt trade confirm the overwhelming importance of trade decentralization on intermediation (Sung 1991, pp. 141–143). Countries that have long histories of trading with China have found it worthwhile to pay for the fixed cost of establishing trade links, and they are less dependent on Hong Kong than new entrants. Political recognition and trade pacts also decrease dependency on Hong Kong. However, the decentralization of China's trading system in 1979 and 1984 has increased the dependency of both old China hands and new entrants on Hong Kong's entrepôt trade. For instance, the dependence of Canada and the United States on Hong Kong for China's exports decreased in the early seventies as they established political and commercial links with China, but this trend reversed in 1979. Starting in 1984, the dependence of all China's major markets (Japan, the United States, Singapore, West Germany, the United Kingdom, Canada, and Australia) on Hong Kong for China's exports increased substantially. Similarly, starting in 1979, all China's major suppliers (Japan, the United States, West Germany, the United Kingdom, France, Italy, and Singapore) became more dependent on Hong Kong for their exports to China.

Efficiency of a Large Trading Hub

China will further decentralize its trading system in the reform process, and Hong Kong's prospects as an entrepôt are bright. There are significant economies of scale and economies of agglomeration in trading activity, and it is very difficult for other cities such as Singapore or Shanghai to compete with Hong Kong, because Hong Kong is the established centre for China's trade. The existence of economies of scale in intermediation would enhance the demand for the middleman, as small firms will not be able to trade efficiently. Yamamura (1976, pp. 184–5) argues that significant economies of scale exist in the production of trading services, as the production of these services usually involves large fixed costs and small or declining marginal costs. In the production of market information, which is part and parcel of intermediation, he argues that considerable costs are involved, and the same market information is useful in many transactions. Moreover, trading firms can also consolidate small orders to efficiently use warehouse and shipping capacities to achieve economies of scale.

Traders tend to agglomerate in a city, suggesting that there are significant external economies involved. This implies that once a city acquires a comparative advantage in trade, the advantage feeds upon itself, and more trading firms will come to the city, making the city even more efficient in trade.

There are in fact external economies on both the demand and supply sides in trade. External economy on the demand side operates through search: an increase in the number of potential trading partners makes trade easier. External economies on the production side are also important in trade. Hicks (1969, pp. 47–49) observes that an increase in the number of merchants in the trading centre will permit specialization and division of labour, not only by lowering costs but also by lowering risks. The larger the number of traders, the easier it is to acquire information, and the easier it is to arrange multilateral contracts or to develop specialized contracts such as insurance and hedging.

Lucas (1985) stresses the importance of agglomeration, especially in service industries, because people in the same trade can interact and learn from one another. He calls this "externality of human capital".

China's Exports Re-exported Elsewhere via Hong Kong

In contrast to the stagnation of China's exports retained in Hong Kong, the growth of its exports re-exported via Hong Kong has been extremely rapid. The share of China's exports re-exported elsewhere via Hong Kong rose from 7.3% in 1979 to a record

49.7% in 1993. The share declined to 38% in 1997, which is still very high.

The rise in the share of China exports re-exported via Hong Kong is clearly related to outward processing. Table 4.3 shows that outward-processing trade dominated Hong Kong's re-exports of China origin and that the proportion of outward-processing trade in Hong Kong's re-exports of China origin rose from 74% in 1991 to 88% in 1997. However, Table 4.3 also shows that the rate of growth of these outward-processing related re-exports slowed from 35.9% in 1992 to 7.6% in 1997. The slowdown is related to Guangdong's rising costs and the spread of industrialization from Guangdong to the North. Guangdong's share in China's exports declined from a peak of 44% in 1994 to 39.7% in 1996 (Table 1.2). The recent decline in the share of China's exports re-exported via Hong Kong is partly related to the relatively slow growth of Guangdong's exports. Another factor is the substitution of direct shipment and transshipment for re-exports, which will be discussed in detail later.

Because of the continuing decentralization of China's trade and the growth of Hong Kong investment in processing operations in China, China's exports via Hong Kong to other countries will continue to grow absolutely. However, relative to China's exports, Hong Kong's share is so large (close to 40%) that it is unlikely to rise further.

China's Imports from Elsewhere via Hong Kong

With China's opening, the share of China's imports imported via Hong Kong (in the form of Hong Kong re-exports) rose from an insignificant 0.5% in 1977 to a record 40.3% in 1997 (Table 4.2).

Outward processing has played an important but declining role in China's imports of Hong re-exports: The proportion of Hong Kong's re-exports to China related to outward processing declined from 50.3% in 1990 to 43.2% in 1996 (Table 4.3) because of China's trade liberalization. Pure entrepôt trade constitutes the bulk of China's imports via Hong Kong. China's increasing reliance on Hong Kong for imports that are not related to outward processing confirms the importance of economies of scale and of agglomeration in entrepôt trade.

Hong Kong's re-exports surpassed its domestic exports in 1988. China has been the foremost market for Hong Kong re-exports since 1980. By 1997 re-exports constituted 85% of Hong Kong's total exports.

Major Commodities Traded and Outward Processing

As over 90% of Hong Kong's imports from China are re-exported, the commodity compositions of imports from China and of re-exports of China origin should be similar. Another factor to consider is the fact that outward-processing trade accounts for the bulk of Hong Kong's trade with China. As the major industries of Hong Kong are clothing and textiles, electronics and electrical equipment, and miscellaneous manufactured goods, the major commodities imported from China should be outputs of these industries. The major commodities exported to China should be inputs of these industries, e.g., yarn or fabric to be processed into textiles and clothing, and electronic components to be assembled into electronic equipment. The major commodities imported from and exported to China should thus be quite similar.

Table 4.4 shows the major commodities in Hong Kong's trade with China in 1996. Electronic and electrical equipment, textiles and clothing, and miscellaneous manufactured articles constituted the bulk of Hong Kong's imports from China, Hong Kong's re-exports of China origin, and Hong Kong's domestic exports to China. In terms of Hong Kong's re-exports to China, miscellaneous manufactured articles were not important, but electronic and electrical equipment and textiles and clothing were. The main commodities imported from and exported to China were indeed quite similar. This is because the bulk of Hong Kong's trade with China is intra-industry trade (exchanges of commodities of the same industry) generated by Hong Kong's investment in China.

Table 4.4
Commodity Composition of Hong Kong's Trade with China, 1996
(%)

Commodity Traded	Domestic Imports from China	Re-export of China Origin	Re-exports to China	Exports to China
Electronic and Electrical Equipment	24.2	27.2	20.5	26.6
Textiles and Clothing	24.1	20.2	16.7	23.0
Miscellaneous Articles Manufactured	13.7	20.1	2.0	6.7
Subtotal	62.0	67.5	39.2	56.3

Source: *Review of Overseas Trade 1996*, Census and Statistics Department, Hong Kong.

The Hong Kong–Guangdong Production Network

Guangdong clearly accounted for the bulk of the outward-processing operations in China. From 1989 to 1996, Hong Kong's imports from Guangdong related to outward processing accounted for 93% to 95% of the imports from China involving outward processing. Hong Kong manufacturers reportedly employed six million workers in Guangdong and only 327,000 workers in Hong Kong (1996 figure). Comparing Hong Kong firms in Guangdong to those in Hong Kong, the gap in employment is 18 to 1, while the gap in exports is only 2.6 to 1. The output gap should be similar to the export gap, as most of the output of Hong Kong manufacturers in Hong Kong and in Guangdong was exported. It is more useful to compare output than employment, partly because Hong Kong workers are more productive than their Guangdong counterparts and partly because workers in firms involved in processing operations in Guangdong do not produce exclusively for their Hong Kong partners. A comparison of value added would be the best measure, but statistics on the value added of Hong Kong operations in Guangdong are not available. The gap in value added is probably smaller than the output gap, as the value added of processing operations tends to be quite low.

Table 4.5

**Hong Kong Exports vs Exports of Hong Kong Firms
in Hong Kong and Guangdong, 1978 and 1996**

	Value (US$ million)		Growth Rate (%)	Market Shares (%)											
				US		China		Japan		EU		Germany		UK	
	1978	1996	78-96	78	96	78	96	78	96	78	96	78	96	78	96
1. Domestic exports	8,690	27,432	6.6	37.2	25.4	0.2	29.0	4.6	5.3	26.7	17.4	10.9	5.4	9.5	5.0
2. Domestic exports of final goods[a]	8,690	21,861	5.3	37.2	31.9	0.2	11.0	4.6	6.7	26.7	21.9	10.9	6.7	9.5	6.3
3. Exports of final goods of HK & Guangdong[b]	8,690	89,766	13.9	37.2	35.7	0.2	2.7	4.6	9.8	26.7	24.9	10.9	6.8	9.5	5.4
4. Total exports	11,507	180,750	16.5	30.3	21.2	0.5	34.3	7.7	6.5	21.7	14.9	8.6	4.2	7.4	3.3
5. Total exports of final goods[c]	11,507	152,004	10.4	30.3	25.2	0.5	21.9	7.7	7.9	21.7	17.7	8.6	5.0	7.4	4.0

Source: *Hong Kong External Trade*, various issues (see Table 4.4 for source).

Notes: (a) Domestic exports of final goods equal domestic exports minus domestic exports to China involving outward processing.

(b) Exports of final goods of H.K. firms in Hong Kong and Guangdong equal domestic exports of final goods plus 0.95 times re-exports of China origin (except to China) involving outward processing. 0.95 is the share of Guangdong in Hong Kong's imports from China related to outward processing. The market composition of Hong Kong's re-exports of Guandong origin involving outward processing is not available, and it is assumed to be the same as that of Hong Kong's re-exports of China origin. For 1995, the former was 81.7% of the latter.

(c) Total exports of final goods equal total exports minus total exports to China involving outward processing.

Adjusting for the Biases of Outward-Processing Trade

In view of the importance of outward-processing trade, Hong Kong's trade statistics should be interpreted with care. One must recognize the special characteristics of outward-processing trade. For instance, China's share in Hong Kong's trade is biased upwards because Hong Kong's domestic exports of semi-manufactured goods to China are re-imported into Hong Kong after processing in China and may even be re-exported to China and re-imported into Hong Kong a few more times before final export to third countries. The overall growth rate and value of Hong Kong's exports and imports are thus also biased upwards. From 1978 to 1996 the value of Hong Kong exports increased at the average rate of 16.5% per year — an extremely high rate of growth. In 1993 Hong Kong overtook Belgium-Luxembourg and the Netherlands to become the world's eighth-largest exporter.

Table 4.5 tries to correct for the biases introduced by outward-processing trade in Hong Kong's export value, growth rates, and the market composition of exports.[1] The first row shows the value, growth rate, and market composition of Hong Kong's *domestic exports*. Domestic exports to China grew rapidly because Hong Kong firms supply their subsidiaries in China with materials and components made in Hong Kong. Hong Kong's domestic exports to China grew from negligible amounts to US$8 billion in 1996, and China surpassed the United States as Hong Kong's foremost market, attracting 29% of domestic exports.

The second row in Table 4.5 shows corresponding statistics for Hong Kong's *domestic exports of final goods* (total domestic exports less domestic exports to China involving outward processing, largely semi-manufactured goods). The value and growth rate of domestic exports of final goods are naturally lower than those of domestic exports. More important, for domestic exports of final goods the decline in the United States' and the European Union's market shares is less dramatic, and the United States is still Hong Kong's foremost market, with 31.9% market share in 1996.

China's 11% share of Hong Kong's domestic exports of final goods is quite large. Because of the recent liberalization of China's imports, Hong Kong exported increasing amounts of final consumer goods to China.

Despite China's import liberalization and the increase in Hong Kong's domestic exports of final goods to China, Hong Kong cannot supply a large variety of products to China, because its manufacturing base is very narrow. Hong Kong specializes in a few light consumer industries, namely clothing, textiles, electronics, toys, plastics, and watches. As has been mentioned before, the share of Hong Kong goods in China's imports declined from record 11.4% in 1990 to 5.7% in 1996 (Tables 4.2a and 4.2b).

The third row in Table 4.5 shows the *exports of final goods of Hong Kong firms* in both Guangdong and Hong Kong. This is equal to the total of *domestic exports of final goods* and Hong Kong's re-exports of goods from outward processing operations in Guangdong, which in turn is 95%[2] of Hong Kong's re-exports of goods from outward-processing operations in China. The value and growth rate of exports of final goods of Hong Kong firms are of course much higher than those of domestic exports. More important, the United States is the foremost market. The share of the U.S. market only declined slightly — from 37% to 35.7% — from 1979 to 1996. The share of the Chinese market was just 2.7%, though this is an understatement because Hong Kong manufacturers in Guangdong can sell part of their output directly in China's domestic market.

The fourth row in Table 4.5 shows Hong Kong's *total exports*, which is the total of domestic exports and re-exports. In 1996 Hong Kong's total exports to China were valued at $US62 billion. Eighty-seven per cent of these were re-exports of third country goods to China, and the rest were Hong Kong's domestic exports. The trend of total exports is dominated by that of re-exports. Both the value and the growth rate of *total* exports are very high, and China was the foremost market of Hong Kong's total exports in 1996. The share of outward-processing trade in total exports to China declined from 59% in 1990 to 47% in 1996 (Table 4.3). The decline occurred once again because of China's import liberalization and the resulting rise in imports of goods not related to outward processing.

The fifth row in Table 4.5 shows *Hong Kong's total exports of final goods*, which is Hong Kong's total exports less its total exports to China related to outward processing. The adjustment is intended to avoid double counting. Unlike in the case of total exports, which shows that China has replaced the United States as Hong Kong's foremost market, the United States is still the top market for total exports of final goods. However, China's 22% market share of total exports of final goods in 1996 was quite high.

To summarize, if we net out trade in semi-manufactured goods between Hong Kong and China, the United States and the European Union are still the largest markets for both Hong Kong products and for the exports of Hong Kong firms in Hong Kong and in Guangdong. However, with import liberalization in China, China is also becoming an important market for final goods.

Table 4.6 shows exports of Hong Kong firms in Hong Kong and Guangdong by commodity. A major share of the exports of many labour-intensive industries are produced from outward-processing operations in Guangdong. These include travel goods and handbags (97.6%), toys (97.6%), telecommunication and sound recording equipment (89.4%), and miscellaneous manufactured goods (86.8%). A smaller proportion of the exports of more skill-intensive industries are produced in Guangdong. These exports include watches and clocks (51.6%), electrical machinery and appliances (59.3%), and office machines and data processing machines (71.9%). Textiles and clothing industries also have a relatively small proportion of their exports produced in Guangdong because exports of textiles and clothing are restricted by quota, and Hong Kong has the largest clothing quota in the world.

Guangdong's Trade with Hong Kong

Guangdong trades a great deal with Hong Kong. This trade accounted for the bulk of Guangdong's trade as well as for the bulk

Chapter 4

Table 4.6

**Exports of Hong Kong Firms by Commodity
and Location of Production, 1996
(US$ million)**

SITC	Commodity Exported	Exports of Hong Kong firms produced in		
		Hong Kong[a]	Guangdong[b]	Total
83	Travel Goods and Handbags	80 3 (2.4)	3,271* (97.6)	3,351 (100)
894	Toys	230 (2.4)	9,547 (97.6)	9,777 (100)
76	Telecommunications and Sound Recording Equipment	1,110 (10.6)	9,340 (89.4)	10,450 (100)
899	Miscellaneous Manufactures	281 (13.2)	1,842* (86.8)	2,123 (100)
69	Metal Manufactures	545 (26.4)	1,519* (73.6)	2,064 (100)
65	Textiles	1,770 (31.6)	3,832* (68.4)	5,602 (100)
75	Office Machines and Automatic Data-Processing Machines	1,693 (28.1)	4,342* (71.9)	6,035 (100)
77	Electrical Machinery and Appliances	3,925 (40.7)	5,714* (59.3)	9,639 (100)
84	Clothing	8,979 (47.3)	9,989 (52.7)	18,968 (100)
885	Watches and Clocks	1,550 (48.4)	1,652* (51.6)	3,202 (100)
Subtotal		20,163 (28.3)	51,048 (71.7)	71,211 (100)
All Commodities		27,432 (28.8)	67,905 (71.2)	95,337 (100)

Source: Census and Statistics Department of Hong Kong.

Notes: Commodities are ranked in descending order of the shares of exports produced in Guangdong

(a) Hong Kong's domestic exports.

(b) Re-exports of Guangdong origin involving outward processing (taken to be 95% of re-exports of China origin involving outward processing).

* Data on re-exports of China origin involving outward processing are not available for these commodities. They are assumed to be equal to 0.95 times 0.818 times Hong Kong's re-exports of China origin of the respective commodities. 0.818 is the average proportion of outward-processing trade in Hong Kong re-exports of China origin for these commodities, while 0.95 is the proportion of Guangdong in Hong Kong's outward-processing trade with China.

of Hong Kong's trade with China in the reform era. In 1996 Hong Kong's imports from Guangdong related to outward processing were valued at US$55.7 billion, accounting for 95% of Hong Kong's imports from China related to outward processing (Table 4.3). Besides exports from processing operations, Guangdong's exports not related to outward processing (exports from "general trade", to use Chinese terminology) were valued at US$12.8 billion, of which at least 80% (US$10.2 billion) were exports to Hong Kong. Guangdong thus accounts for around 70% of Hong Kong's other imports from China not related to outward processing, and Hong Kong's total imports from Guangdong in 1996 were worth at least US$65.9 billion (90% of Hong Kong's imports from China).

As for Hong Kong's exports to Guangdong, Hong Kong's 1996 exports to China related to outward processing were valued at US$28.7 billion, of which around 95%[3] should be destined for Guangdong. On top of this, we have to add a substantial amount not related to outward processing. In 1996 Hong Kong's exports to Guangdong accounted for the bulk of Guangdong's imports, worth US$50.6 billion, as well as for the bulk of Hong Kong's total exports to China, worth US$62 billion.

China's Service Trade with Hong Kong

Service trade between the Mainland and Hong Kong is extremely important. Conceptually, the re-export margin that Hong Kong earns through entrepôt trade in fact represents export of services. However, such services are embodied in the price of goods sold and are thus usually recorded in trade statistics as export of goods rather than as export of services.

Hong Kong visitors accounted for roughly 60% of tourist arrivals as well as for tourist expenditure in China in the mid-1990s. Hong Kong also exports transportation services, trading services, construction services, financial services, and business services to China. However, reliable data is lacking for categories other than entrepôt trade and tourism. Hong Kong's export of financial services to China is undoubtedly substantial, as Hong Kong and

Table 4.7
China's Transshipment of Goods through Hong Kong, 1983–96
(thousand tonnes)

Year	From China		To China	
	Transshipment	Direct Shipment	Transshipment	Direct Shipment
1983	784 (23.7)	3,312	102 (66.3)	154
1984	883 (28.9)	3,056	300 (50.3)	595
1985	1,046 (41.1)	2,544	1,043 (95.7)	1,090
1986	1,538 (42.3)	3,636	829 (79.2)	1,047
1987	1,810 (41.0)	4,415	1,270 (178.8)	711
1988	1,946 (47.4)	4,107	1,548 (116.9)	1,324
1989	2,123 (49.3)	4,308	1,356 (68.5)	1,981
1990	2,195 (43.8)	5,008	924 (54.4)	1,697
1991	2,379 (50.4)	4,720	1,625 (65.6)	2,478
1992	2,547 (49.3)	5,166	1,741 (54.4)	3,201
1993	3,363 (63.4)	5,308	2,048 (64.3)	3,183
1994	4,573 (90.8)	5,039	3,147 (79.6)	3,953
1995	5,252 (98.5)	5,330	4,190 (85.1)	4,924
1996	4,304 (83.1)	5,177	4,486 (79.6)	5,638
1997	4,409 (94.5)	4,666	4,882 (82.1)	5,944

Source: *Hong Kong Shipping Statistics*, Census and Statistics Department, Hong Kong, various issues.

Note: Figures in brackets are percentage of transshipment over direct shipment of goods.

China are each other's foremost partners in investment. Hong Kong is the foremost base for China consultancy and legal services.

Hong Kong is also the number one gateway for foreigners touring China. Many foreigners join package tours of China organized in Hong Kong. Though China is establishing more direct air links with other countries, the percentage of foreign tourists leaving China via Hong Kong has been going up since 1982. It rose to 55% in 1987. This paradox is explained by China's decentralization of the authority to organize China tours from the China Travel Service to provincial and local authorities in the early 1980s. Decentralization increases search costs and the demand for intermediation. Taiwan lifted its ban on travel to the Mainland in 1987, and this of course led to another jump in the number of foreigners visiting China via Hong Kong.

In commodity trade, Hong Kong is an important entrepôt as well as a centre of transshipment for China. Transshipment means that goods are consigned directly from the exporting country to a buyer in the importing country, though the goods are transported via Hong Kong and usually change vessel in Hong Kong. Chinese goods, for example, are carried by train or coastal vessels to Hong Kong, where they are consolidated into containers for ocean shipping. Unlike re-exports (entrepôt trade) transshipment is not regarded as part of Hong Kong's trade, as there is no Hong Kong buyer. The government does not collect statistics on the value of transshipments, as they do not go through Hong Kong customs, though their weight and volume are known from cargo statistics.

Table 4.7 shows China's transshipment via Hong Kong. Statistics on China–Hong Kong direct shipments (which represent China–Hong Kong trade) are shown for comparison. China's transshipment via Hong Kong has increased much faster than China–Hong Kong direct shipments. In 1983, the first year for which statistics on transshipment are available, Hong Kong transshipment of goods from China constituted only 24% of direct shipment from China (which represents imports from China). By 1995 transshipment of goods from China was nearly equal to direct shipment. The transshipment of goods to China has also grown extremely rapidly. Both by weight and by volume, China's transshipment via Hong Kong in 1995 was about as large as were China–Hong Kong direct shipments, which constituted the bulk of China–Hong Kong trade.

Besides dealing with re-exports and transshipment, Hong Kong traders also perform a brokerage role in a substantial portion of China's direct trade. This is called "offshore trade" because the Hong Kong firm acts as a middleman between offshore production bases and overseas customers.

From surveys conducted on Hong Kong's traders (Hong Kong Trade Development Council 1998), it is known that an overwhelming (but falling) portion of their sales of Chinese products was re-exported via Hong Kong. From 1992 to 1997 re-exports' share declined from 81% to 72%, while the shares of transshipment and offshore trade shipped directly from China have increased to 12.4% and 15.8%, respectively, from 11% and 8%, respectively.

For sales of third country (non-Chinese) products of the surveyed traders from 1992 to 1997, Re-exports' share dropped from 52% to 40.4%. Transshipment's share also declined from 12.2% to 7.7%, while the share of offshore trade rose sharply, from 36% to 52%. For Hong Kong companies selling both Chinese and third-country products, there has clearly been a substitution of offshore trade for re-exports. This is because China recently liberalized foreign investment in shipping and cargo forwarding, and foreign firms have found it easier to handle Chinese trade through transshipment and offshore trade bypassing Hong Kong.

The share of China's trade handled by Hong Kong is appreciably larger than that reflected by re-exports, as the goods handled by Hong Kong traders through transshipment and offshore trade (direct shipment bypassing Hong Kong) should be included. In 1997 the shares of Chinese exports consumed, re-exported, transshipped, and directly shipped by Hong Kong were 3.1%, 38.0%, 6.6%, and 8.4%, respectively, totalling 55.5%. Hong Kong thus plays an important role in over half of China's exports. On the import side, the shares of China's imports transshipped, and directly shipped by Hong Kong cannot be estimated from the survey as third country products are sold by Hong Kong firms to China as well as elsewhere. Nevertheless, as Hong Kong already produced and re-exported 46% of China's imports in 1997, Hong Kong would handle the bulk of China's imports of transshipment and offshore trade were included.

China's export of services to Hong Kong has increased rapidly in recent years. China's construction firms are active in construction projects in Hong Kong. A large number of mainland Chinese are working in Hong Kong, including manufacturing workers imported to relieve the labour shortage in Hong Kong and engineers working in China-owned factories in Hong Kong. Hong Kong residents have also travelled to China for medical treatment because the price of health care is lower there. Conversely, many mainland Chinese have travelled to Hong Kong to seek higher-quality medical treatment.

Notes

1. Such adjustments have first been made in the *Economic Report* of the Hongkong Bank, January 1991.

2. This is Guangdong's share of Hong Kong's imports involving outward processing from China.

3. See note 2.

CHAPTER 5

Hong Kong–China Investments

Hong Kong's Investment in China

Hong Kong investment in China is diversified, ranging from small-scale, labour-intensive operations to large-scale infrastructure projects. The primary motivation of Hong Kong investment in China is economic rather than political. In Hong Kong, most manufacturing firms are small, and thousands of them have been investing in China since the mid-1980s. Hong Kong's big firms are mostly in the service sector (banks, real estate, shipping, aviation), and they were not active investors in China before Deng's southern tour of 1992. However, some of them made donations to China in return for political goodwill. This is simply because the Chinese investment environment was not favourable for investors in the service sector. Unlike manufacturing output, which can be exported and sold for foreign exchange, services are usually sold on the domestic market for Renminbi, which are not convertible, and the foreign investor had a problem recouping his investment. Moreover, China did not liberalize foreign investment in services until 1992.

Before 1992, instead of investing in China, many of Hong Kong's big firms invested overseas to diversify their portfolio away from Hong Kong and China as insurance against the planned Chinese take-over. However, investment in alien turf is tricky, and many of the investments were not very profitable. After Deng's southern tour in 1992, a large number of Hong Kong's big firms quickly grasped their opportunity and spearheaded the tide of external investment in China. Deng's tour stimulated a wave of investment by major Hong Kong companies, including listed

Table 5.1
Utilized Foreign Direct Investment in China by Destination, 1979–96
(US$ million)

Year	National Total	Guangdong	From Hong Kong in		
			China	Guangdong	Shanghai
1979–85	4,723	1,801	3,020	1,500	108
	(100)	(38.1)	(63.9)	(31.8)	(2.3)
1986	1,874	723	1,115	625	148
	(100)	(38.6)	(59.5)	(33.4)	(7.9)
1987	2,314	603	1,588	513	214
	(100)	(26.1)	(68.6)	(22.2)	(9.2)
1988	3,194	958	2,068	775	233
	(100)	(30.0)	(64.7)	(24.3)	(7.3)
1989	3,392	1,156	2,037	953	442
	(100)	(34.1)	(60.1)	(28.1)	(13.0)
1990	3,487	1,460	1,880	996	174
	(100)	(41.9)	(53.9)	(28.6)	(5.0)
1991	4,366	1,823	2,405	1,356	145
	(100)	(41.8)	(55.1)	(31.1)	(3.3)
1992	11,008	3,552	7,507	3,069	481
	(100)	(32.3)	(68.2)	(27.9)	(4.4)
1993	27,515	7,498	17,275	6,530	3,160
	(100)	(27.3)	(62.8)	(23.7)	(11.5)
1994	33,767	9,397	19,665	7,768	2,473
	(100)	(27.8)	(58.2)	(23.0)	(7.3)
1995	37,521	10,180	20,060	7,973	2,893
	(100)	(27.1)	(53.5)	(21.2)	(7.7)
1979–95	133,159	39,151	78,620	32,058	10,471
	(100)	(29.4)	(59.0)	(24.1)	(7.9)
1996	41,726	11,624	20,677	8,387	3,941
	(100)	(27.9)	(49.6)	(20.1)	(9.4)
1979–96	174,885	50,775	99,297	40,445	14,412
	(100)	(29.0)	(56.8)	(23.1)	(8.2)

Sources: FDI of Hong Kong in Guangdong: Zhang, Wang, and Chen (1997), Table 3; other data come from *Almanac of China's Foreign Relations and Trade*, various issues.

Note: Figures in brackets are row percentages.

companies such as Cheung Kong, Hutchison-Whampoa, Sun Hung Kai Properties, New World, and Kowloon Wharf, in projects ranging from real estate to infrastructure and commerce.

Hong Kong also became the major funding centre for Chinese firms. A number of China investment funds that invested in B shares in Chinese stock markets in the early 1990s were established.

In 1992 China approved the public listing of selective state enterprises in the Hong Kong stock market. Their shares are commonly called H-shares. Besides tapping external funds, listing in Hong Kong also speeds up China's enterprise reforms, since listed firms have to follow international accounting standards. By the end of 1994 fifteen such stocks were listed in Hong Kong, with a market capitalization of US$1.8 billion (Ni 1994, p. 20). Together with forty listed Hong Kong companies controlled by China, the aggregate capitalization was about 4% of the Hong Kong market (Ni 1994, p. 10). By the end of May 1997 the number of H-shares has risen to twenty-four, with a market capitalization of US$6.9 billion or around 1% of Hong Kong's stock market. The number of listed Hong Kong companies controlled by mainland Chinese shareholders rose to around fifty, with a market capitalization of US$49 billion or 10% of Hong Kong's stock market. The Hang Seng Bank introduced a China-Affiliated Corporations Index or Red Chips Index on 16 June 1997.

Hong Kong's Investment in Guangdong

Table 5.1 shows utilized FDI in Guangdong and in Shanghai as well as Hong Kong's investment in Guangdong. From 1979 to 1996 Guangdong accounted for close to 30% of the FDI in China. Hong Kong accounted for 80% of the FDI in Guangdong, and Guangdong accounted for 41% of Hong Kong's FDI in China.

While Guangdong has consistently been the leading Chinese province in attracting FDI, its share of the national total has fluctuated from a peak of close to 42% in 1990 to a low of 28% in 1996. Guangdong's share was usually high when the investment environment in China was not so good, and its share usually declined with an improvement in the Chinese investment environment, as foreign investors spread out from Guangdong to other provinces.

In the early years of China's opening, from 1979 to 1985, Guangdong had 38% of the FDI in China, while Shanghai's share was only 2.3%. This was the period during which China had just started to attract foreign investment, and there were naturally many of problems with the Chinese investment environment.

China's investment environment improved in 1987 after the implementation of the twenty-two-point investment enticement package announced in October 1986. Guangdong's share of China's FDI declined somewhat, and Shanghai's share rose rapidly in the late 1980s, reaching a peak of 13% in 1989, while Guangdong's share was 34%.

However, China's investment environment suffered heavily as a result of the Tiananmen incident of 1989. Pudong was declared open in early 1990, partly to demonstrate China's determination to continue its policy of opening and reform, but international investors remained sceptical, and Shanghai's share dropped to a low of 3% in 1991. In contrast, Guangdong's share of China's FDI reached a record high of 42% in the same year. This reflects the fact that Guangdong was able to resist the conservative policies sweeping the rest of China.

Deng's 1992 southern tour led to a dramatic improvement in the investment environment and a quantum jump in FDI, and Guangdong's share in China's FDI declined. However, in 1996 Guangdong's 28% share of China's FDI was still nearly three times Shanghai's share of 9.4%. Despite the rebound in Shanghai's share starting in 1992, Shanghai's 1996 share was still lower than its 1989 record of 13%.

It must be stressed that Hong Kong's investment in Guangdong is very large. In 1995, US$8 billion of Guangdong's US$ 10.2 billion of utilized FDI came from Hong Kong, exceeding total inward FDI of US$7 billion in Mexico, which was the world's number two recipient of FDI among developing countries. The 1993 contracted FDI in Guangdong (US$33.1 billion) exceeded that in the entire ASEAN (US$17.3 billion)! In 1993 China and Guangdong attracted so much FDI that capital inflows into ASEAN decreased. This drop in FDI reinforced ASEAN governments' desire to set up the Northern and Eastern Growth Triangles[1] to attract FDI. The impact of Greater Hong Kong on East Asia and the world is beyond dispute.

Distribution of Hong Kong's Investment in Guangdong by Industry

The distribution of Hong Kong's investment in Guangdong by industry, which was not released until 1997, is shown in Table 5.2. As Hong Kong accounts for 80% of the FDI in Guangdong, the distribution of FDI in Guangdong by industry is similar to that shown in Table 5.2.

Industrial investment has consistently accounted for over 70% of Hong Kong's FDI in Guangdong. The industrial share was over 80% from 1988 to 1992 but declined thereafter with China's liberalization of foreign investment in services after Deng's 1992 southern tour. The share of services rose from 16% in 1992 to 27% in 1993 and rose further to 30% in 1995. Investments in real estate accounted for the bulk of the FDI in services. The share of transportation and communications rose from 0.7% in 1992 to 4.5% in 1995, showing the rise in importance of infrastructure investment.

Benefits of Foreign Investment for China

There is mounting evidence that foreign investment's contribution to China's growth is substantial. As has been mentioned before, foreign investment, especially that from Hong Kong and Taiwan, is the crux of China's spectacular export drive. The share of FDI in China's gross domestic investment rose from 4.5% in 1991 to 18.3% in 1994 (United Nations, 1996).

Econometric tests have been done on the contribution of foreign investment compared with domestic investment to growth in China, and foreign investment appears to contribute much more (Qiu 1996, Wei 1995). In Qiu's work, which is the best that has

Chapter 5

Table 5.2

Foreign Direct Investment from Hong Kong in Guangdong by Industry, 1979–95
(US$ million)

Year	Total	Primary Sector	Secondary Sector		Tertiary Sector			
			Industry	Cons-truction	Real Estate	Transport and Commu-nication	Others	Sub-total
1979–84	1,035	19.7	772	22	153	30	38	221
	(100)	(1.9)	(74.6)	(2.1)	(14.8)	(2.9)	(3.7)	(21.4)
1985	467	9.0	348	9.8	69	14	17	100
	(100)	(1.9)	(24.6)	(2.1)	(14.8)	(2.9)	(3.7)	(21.4)
1986	625	12	466	13	93	18	23	134
	(100)	(1.9)	(74.6)	(2.1)	(14.8)	(2.9)	(3.7)	(21.4)
1987	513	13	399	17	57	8.2	18	83
	(100)	(2.5)	(278)	(3.4)	(11.2)	(1.6)	(3.4)	(16.2)
1988	775	18	625	13	78	22	18	118
	(100)	(2.4)	(80.7)	(1.2)	(10.1)	(2.9)	(2.3)	(15.3)
1989	953	18	783	2.2	103	22	24	149
	(100)	(1.9)	(82.2)	(0.2)	(10.8)	(2.3)	(2.5)	(15.6)
1990	996	9.0	830	0.58	92	13	52	157
	(100)	(0.9)	(83.4)	(0.1)	(9.2)	(1.3)	(5.2)	(15.7)
1991	1,355	12	1,124	3.2	169	25	22	216
	(100)	(0.9)	(82.9)	(0.2)	(12.5)	(1.9)	(1.6)	(16.0)
1992	3,069	31	2,527	29	420	22	40	482
	(100)	(1.0)	(82.3)	(0.9)	(13.7)	(0.7)	(1.3)	(5.7)
1993	6,530	30	4,659	73	134	185	241	560
	(100)	(0.5)	(71.4)	(1.1)	(20.6)	(2.8)	(3.7)	(27.1)
1994	7,767	57	5,567	149	1556	211	227	1,994
	(100)	(0.7)	(71.7)	(1.9)	(20.0)	(2.7)	(3.0)	(25.7)
1995	7,973	66	5,152	339	1606	356	454	2,416
	(100)	(0.8)	(64.6)	(4.3)	(20.1)	(4.5)	(5.7)	(30.3)
1979–95	32,058	295	23,253	671	5739	926	1174	7,839
	(100)	(0.9)	(72.5)	(2.1)	(17.9)	(2.9)	(3.7)	(24.5)

Source: Zhang, Wang, and Chen (1997), Table 6.
Note: Figures in brackets are row percentages.

been done so far, the marginal product of FDI (extra output produced by one additional unit of investment) was 0.466, whereas the marginal product of domestic investment was only 0.165 (Qiu 1996, p. 65).

According to the works just mentioned, exports also benefit China's growth substantially. Qiu has found that exports have significant spillover effects for the non-export sector. An increase of exports by 1% raises the output of the non-export sector by 0.037% (Qiu 1996, p. 58).

Though foreign investment and exports have undoubtedly brought tremendous benefits to China, it appears that the remnants of China's planned system have significantly limited the level of these benefits that would have accrued to China. For instance, it is known that the rate-of-processing margin of China's processed exports (from processing operations or from foreign-invested enterprises) was 20% or less from 1990 to 1995 (using the value of processed exports as the base), whereas the profit margin and re-export margin earned by Hong Kong was as high as one-third of the value of exports.[2] In China's processed exports, the "take" of Hong Kong investors and traders is much higher than that of Chinese manufacturers.

Hong Kong's "take" is relatively high because Hong Kong performs a lot of value-adding services for processing operations in China, including product design, marketing or order taking from importers, sourcing, quality control, trade financing and co-ordination of shipping. Hong Kong investors in China often use transfer pricing to transfer the profits of their subsidiaries back to Hong Kong to evade Chinese controls, and such profits also appear as part of the re-export mark-up.

The fact that China is dependent on Hong Kong for so many of the above services shows the weakness of the Chinese system. China's firms are dependent on Hong Kong's trade financing because of the system of credit rationing in China, which favours state-owned enterprises. China depends on external investors to perform international marketing and order taking from importers, partly because it is cumbersome for Chinese nationals to get passports to travel overseas.

Processing operations and foreign-invested enterprises tend to import most of their raw materials because it is difficult to depend on the quality or reliability of local suppliers. The rigidity of China's economic system hampers the development of forward and backward linkages to local enterprises and thus limit the potential benefits of foreign investment. However, the rate of processing margin increased to 26% in 1996 and 41% in 1997. This probably indicates that economic reforms have increased the flexibility of the Chinese economy.

History of China's Investment in Hong Kong

China was an important investor in Hong Kong in the pre-reform era, as Hong Kong was China's gateway to the capitalist world. As has been mentioned, Hong Kong was the largest market for China in the late 1960s and early 1970s. China's investment in Hong Kong was designed to enhance China's foreign exchange earnings from Hong Kong through exports and remittances. China's business interests were represented by four large conglomerates, namely the Bank of China (BOC) and its twelve sister banks, the China Resources Company, the China Merchants Company, and China Travel Service.

China's investments in Hong Kong were conservative. They were designed to handle, transport, and finance China's exports to Hong Kong and also to handle remittances and visitors. They did not take advantage of local business opportunities. For instance, the BOC Group confined itself largely to China-related trade financing and remittances. The China Resource Company distributed Chinese products, as it was the sole agent of China's exports to Hong Kong. The Group has many subsidiaries specializing in retail trade, including China Arts and Crafts and many department stores selling Chinese products. A pro-China 1981 economic yearbook listed some 1,136 sub-agents or wholesalers and 101 department stores specializing in Chinese products (Jao 1983, p. 45). The China

Merchants Company shipped China-related trade, and China Travel Service handled overseas visitors to China. In support of its propaganda effort, China also invested in publishing, book stores, magazines, news agencies, and motion picture production and distribution in Hong Kong. In the reform era, Chinese investment has been much more aggressive, as will be discussed in detail in the following section.

Size of Chinese Investment in Hong Kong

As is mentioned in Chapter 1, China has been one of the top investors among developing economies. Hong Kong is the destination for over 80% of its outward FDI.

In May 1996 the Hong Kong government published the first surveys (1993 and 1994) of external investment in Hong Kong's non-manufacturing sectors (Census and Statistics Department, Hong Kong, 1996b), and these give the first precise data on external investment in Hong Kong. Since then the 1995 and 1996 surveys have been published. At the end of 1995 China's stock of FDI in Hong Kong was US$12.4 billion. China was the second-largest external investor in Hong Kong, with a 17.9% share, after the United Kingdom (28.2%) but ahead of Japan (17.2%) and the United States (12.1%).

The aforementioned surveys reveal that previous estimates of Chinese investment in Hong Kong were exaggerated. These estimates put Chinese investment at US$20 billion or US$25 billion by 1994 or 1995.[3]

China's investment in Hong Kong is very diversified, covering nearly all sectors of the Hong Kong economy, namely banking, insurance, entrepôt trade, shipping, aviation, real estate, and manufacturing. China's investment strengthens the ties of Hong Kong to China and enhances the position of Hong Kong as the gateway to China.

The "round tripping" of Chinese capital in Hong Kong (Chinese capital that flows to Hong Kong and then back to China to be recorded as foreign investment in order to capture the benefits

Table 5.3

Distribution of Number of Chinese Companies in Hong Kong by Industry, 1991

Industries that China's Companies are in	Share of the Industries
Manufacturing and related investment	11.5%
Construction and real estate management	6.9%
Import and export	38.8%
Tourism	3.5%
Transportation and storage	8.5%
Finance and insurance	10.4%
Others (holding companies or non-business administrative organizations)	20.4%
Total	100%

Source: 1991 Report of the Association of Hong Kong Chinese Enterprises.

given to foreign investors) inflates both the figures of Chinese investment in Hong Kong and those of Hong Kong investment in China. Unfortunately, the precise amounts are very difficult to estimate.

China's Investment by Industry

The 1991 annual report of the Hong Kong Chinese Enterprises Association lists the distribution by industry of its 922 corporate members (Table 5.3). The information is of limited value, as it pertains to the number of firms rather than to the value of investment. Moreover, only a small portion of Chinese companies in Hong Kong are members of the association. The information was released only for 1991 but not for subsequent years.

According to the limited information released, 39% of the Chinese companies in Hong Kong were in import and export which was by far the leading recipient. This is expected as Hong Kong is the foremost trading hub of China. Manufacturing was a distant second, with 11.5% of Chinese companies. Finance and insurance and transportation and storage were close behind, in third and fourth places, with 10.4% and 8.5%, respectively, of Chinese companies. Transportation and storage are obviously trade related. The importance of finance and insurance in Chinese investment in Hong Kong is expected given the long history of the BOC Group and the importance of Hong Kong as an international financial centre.

China's Economic Presence in Major Sectors of Hong Kong's Economy

Table 5.4 summarizes China's economic presence in major sectors of the Hong Kong economy. Chinese companies are important in Hong Kong in the areas of import–export, banking, insurance, manufacturing, shipping, real estate, and tourism.

Chinese companies, led by the China Resources Group, handled around 20% of Hong Kong's trade in 1993. As China accounted for 36% of Hong Kong's trade in 1996, the prominence of Chinese companies in trade is expected.

The BOC and its twelve "sister banks" have long been the cornerstone of Chinese investment in Hong Kong. China now has fifteen banks in Hong Kong, as the CITIC (China International Trust and Investment Company) acquired the Ka Wah Bank and the China Merchants Group acquired the Union Bank in 1986. The BOC joined the Hong Kong Bank and the Standard Chartered Bank as the third note-issuing bank in Hong Kong in May 1994.

The BOC Group is the second-largest banking group in Hong Kong, after the Hong Kong Bank Group. It had a 23% share of deposits and an 11% share of total banking assets in 1996. In terms of banking assets, it was in the fourth place, after Japanese banks, the Hong Kong Bank Group, and European banks. However, Japanese and Europeans banks operate individually rather than in a group. In 1996, though Japanese banks had 44% of all banking assets, they had only 3.5% of all Hong Kong dollar deposits. Their loans were mainly used outside Hong Kong. Japanese banks are mainly involved in the international financial market rather than the local market. The Hong Kong Bank Group and the BOC Group have long dominated the local market.

Table 5.4

China's Economic Presence in Hong Kong by Economic Sector

Sector	Value / Volume	As share of Hong Kong's Total	Rank
Imports / Exports[a]	1993 Trade value of US$54 billion	20%	First among external investors
Banking[b]	1996 Assets of US$112 billion	11%	Fourth
	1996 Deposits of US$73 billion	23%	Second after the Hong Kong Bank Group
Insurance[c]		20% of market for general insurance	—
Manufacturing[d]	1995 Cumulative investment of US$388 million	7% of external investment	Third after Japan and the United States
Shipping[e]		10% of throughput from 1992 to 1994	—
Real Estate[f]	1993 Transactions worth US$1.3 billion to US$1.9 billion	20%–30% of property transactions	—
Hotels[f]		8.3% of 33,297 hotel rooms in April 1992	—

Sources: (a) Liu Qingwen, "Hong Kong PRC-Invested Enterprises: Before and After 1997", *The Hong Kong Chinese Enterprise*, Autumn 1994, pp. 39–44.
(b) Hong Kong Monetary Authority, *Annual Report*, 1996
(c) Includes only insurance of China Insurance Holdings Company. See Wang Xianzhang, "Expand Insurance Business at an Accelerated Speed", *The Hong Kong Chinese Enterprise*, Autumn 1994, pp. 50–53.
(d) Hong Kong Government Industry Department, *1996 Survey of External Investment in Hong Kong's Manufacturing Industries*, 1996.
(e) Includes only shipping of China Merchants Holdings Group. Information obtained from interview.
(f) Ni, Nick, "China's Expanding Economic Interests in Hong Kong", *Asian Perspectives*, Nomura Research Institute (Hong Kong), 11: p. 6, December 1994.

The BOC Group has been very innovative. In Hong Kong, it pioneered the introduction of deposits in European Currency Units, telephone banking, and the use of a single passbook for nineteen foreign currency deposits. The BOC Group has also established branches in China and pioneered the introduction of mortgage loans. Much useful information and many valuable innovations have been transmitted from the BOC Group to China, thus facilitating China's banking and economic reforms. On the other hand, Hong Kong's rise as a financial centre also owes a lot to the modernization and internationalization of the BOC Group.

The China Insurance Holdings Company, a subsidiary of the People's Insurance Company of China, is reported in 1994 to claim a 20% share of Hong Kong's market for general insurance (Wang 1994, p. 50). Though the company has been quite successful in the area of general insurance, its share of the life insurance market is small. Provincial and local authorities also run subsidiary insurance companies in Hong Kong (Shen 1993, p. 436). The Insurance Committee of the Hong Kong Chinese Enterprises Association has a membership of fifteen companies.

Chinese investment in manufacturing is quite modest, and China's share of the stock of external investment in Hong Kong manufacturing declined from 18% in 1985 to 7% in 1995. In 1995 China was a distant third, after Japan (39%) and the United States (28.5%), and Chinese investment in manufacturing made up only 2.8% of total Chinese investment in Hong Kong. As Hong Kong is primarily a service centre for China, and China's labour costs are much lower than those of Hong Kong, the modest scale of China's involvement in Hong Kong manufacturing is not surprising.

As has been mentioned before, many Chinese companies have invested in shipping, transportation, and tourism in Hong Kong. The figure on shipping in Table 5.4 pertains only to the China Merchants Group, accounting for around 10% of the total throughput from 1992 to 1994. China Merchants had a fleet totalling over six million tons of dead weight and assets of over HK$40 billion in 1994.[4] The China Resource Group had a fleet of more than fifty cargo ships in 1994 (Ni 1994, p. 14). Besides their investments in shipping and transportation, the China Merchants Group, China Resources, China Travel Service, and Guangdong Enterprise also have extensive interests in tourism and hotels. There

Table 5.5
Chinese Companies in Hong Kong, by Supervisory Level of Government
(End of 1993)

Type of Control	No. of Firms	Supervisory Government Body of China
State controlled	50	State Council and ministries
Provincial controlled	72	Provinces and municipalities
Local controlled	530	City government or below
Agent "window"	13,300	Various local governments
Military backed	18	Various military authorities

Source: Ni (1994, p. 5). (see note f, Table 5.4)

were thirty-six mainland tourism companies in Hong Kong in 1992, and Chinese companies owned 8.3% of the total 33,297 hotel rooms in Hong Kong (Ni 1994, p. 14).

Chinese companies started to invest in Hong Kong property in the 1980s, beginning with the fifty-storey headquarters of the Chinese Resource Company. In the late 1980s unofficial Chinese companies cashed in on the real estate boom in Hong Kong through speculation, though this was prohibited by Beijing. George Shen made detailed counts of Chinese investment in Hong Kong property, basing his results on newspaper reports. Total Chinese investment between 1988 and 1991 was valued at US$941 million; for 1992 the figure was US$109 million, and the total for the first five months of 1993 was US$643 million (Shen 1993, p. 437). Ni's estimate for 1993 was US$1.3 to 1.9 billion, or 20% to 30% of the property transactions that took place in Hong Kong (Ni 1994, p. 12). In the real estate sector, China has probably risen to first place among external investors.

Organization and Operation of Chinese Companies in Hong Kong

Chinese companies are controlled by the Chinese government through the appointment of mainland cadres to top positions. The

New China News Agency (NCNA), China's de facto embassy in Hong Kong before Hong Kong's reversion, oversees Chinese companies in Hong Kong. However, the NCNA has not been able to effectively control companies linked to the military, companies associated with "princelings" (children of top leaders), and unofficial companies financed by local governments (Ni 1994, p. 4). Some well-known companies affiliated with municipal (city) governments have refused to acknowledge their connections and refuse to join the Association of Hong Kong Chinese Enterprises (Sung 1996, p. 13).

Table 5.5 gives Ni's estimate of the number of Chinese companies affiliated with various levels of the Chinese government (Ni 1994, p. 5). Fifty of the companies are controlled by the State Council or its ministries. Seventy-two companies representing provincial and municipal (city) governments have been officially approved, while an estimated 530 companies affiliated with municipal (city) or local authorities operate unofficially in Hong Kong. Though officially approved companies are under the purview of the NCNA, provincial and municipal companies enjoy a lot more autonomy than state-run companies (Ni 1994, p. 6). They do not need to remit profits to the central government.

It should be noted that companies operated by provincial or municipal governments can be very large. For instance, Guangdong Enterprises, which is operated by the Guangdong provincial government, has assets equalling those of CITIC (Hong Kong), which amounted to HK$20 billion at the end of 1993. The Yue Xiu Group of the Guangzhou municipal government had assets worth HK$5 billion at the end of 1993.

Ni estimates that the number of agents functioning as "windows" of local governments in Hong Kong totalled 13,300 in 1994 (Table 5.5). He apparently assumes that one-third of the 40,000 foreign-invested enterprises in China owned by Hong Kong functioned as agent "windows" for local governments (Sung 1996, p. 23).

Ni estimates that there were eighteen companies, including the China Poly Group and the China Aerospace Corporation, with

Table 5.6
Major "Princeling Companies" in Hong Kong (Known to the Public)

Company Name	Person in Charge	Family Links
CITIC (HK)	Larry **Yung**	Son of **Rong** Yiren, VP of PRC
Continental Mariner	**Wang** Jun	Son of **Wang** Zhen, VP of PRC
China Poly Group	**He** Ping	Son-in-law of **Deng** Xiaoping
First Shanghai	**Chen** Weili	Daughter of **Chen** Yun, influential leader
Ong Group (China Venturetech)	**Chen** Weili	Daughter of **Chen** Yun, influential leader
Guangdong Investment (Guangdong Enterprises)	**Ye** Weiping	Son of **Ye** Xuanping, VP of CPPCC
Laws Property (CNNC)	**Song** Kefang	Son of **Song** Renqiong, influential leader
Kader Investment	**Deng** Zifang	Youngest son of **Deng** Xiaoping
CNNC	**Wu** Jiangchang	Eldest son-in-law of **Deng** Xiaoping

Source: Ni (1994, p. 8), (see note f, Table 5.4).
Note: Surnames are in boldface.

military backing operating in Hong Kong in 1993 and that their assets totalled around HK$10 billion (Ni 1994, p. 7). The China Poly Group was founded in 1984 by military authorities and was the largest arms trader of the People's Liberation Army (PLA). Its holdings in Hong Kong included interests in shipping and property investment (Ni 1994, p. 21). China Aerospace Corporation specializes in high-tech aerospace products. It manufactures the "Long March" rockets that propel commercial satellites into orbit.

The major "princeling companies" in Hong Kong as listed by Ni are shown in Table 5.6. They include some of the most powerful Chinese companies in Hong Kong, such as CITIC (HK), Laws Property, Continental Mariner of the China Poly Group, Ong Group of the China Venturetech, and Guangdong Investment of Guangdong Enterprises. The business elite of Hong Kong often strengthen their relationship with the Chinese leadership by helping the princelings to acquire listed companies in Hong Kong. For instance, Hong Kong magnate Li Ka-shing joined hands with Deng Zifang (the youngest son of Deng Xiaoping) and the Shougang Corporation to acquire Kader investment.

The memoirs of Xu Jiatun, the former head of the NCNA, contain interesting references to Chinese enterprises in Hong Kong. Xu complained about the difficulty of managing Chinese companies in Hong Kong, especially the princeling companies, which have the personal support of central leaders. Xu remarked that he was powerless to investigate into the irregularities of CITIC (HK), and the China Everbright Company, then under the chairmanship of Wang Guanying, brother-in-law of former State President Liu Shaoqi (Xu 1993, pp. 259–261). Xu knew of around 200 children of high-ranking cadres doing business in Hong Kong (Xu 1993, p. 261). He mentioned two cases of rampant corruption. In one case, Beijing wanted to transfer the person involved back to the Mainland, but he emigrated to Australia. In another case, Xu's complaints were ignored, and the person involved continued to make big money in Hong Kong (Xu 1993, p. 262).

Determinants of Chinese Investment in Hong Kong

In the open-door era economic factors are paramount in Chinese investment in Hong Kong, though political factors are still important. Hong Kong is the destination of 80% of China's outward investment because Hong Kong is *the* gateway of China. Hong Kong's role as China's gateway can be analyzed according to four main functions (Sung 1991, p. 17): those of financier, trading partner, middleman, and facilitator (Table 5.7). China's investment in Hong Kong can be analyzed according to these functions.

Hong Kong as Financier

Hong Kong's share of foreign direct investment in China has been around 60% throughout the open-door era. Many Chinese provincial and local authorities have set up offices in Hong Kong to attract

Table 5.7
Role of Hong Kong as China's Gateway

Hong Kong's Role as	Role Functions	Gateway Activities
Financier	Direct investment, Indirect investment, Loan syndication	
Trading partner	Commodity trade, Services trade	
Middleman	Commodity trade	Entrepôt trade, Transshipment, Brokerage in direct trade
	Services trade	Tourism, Loan syndication, Business consultancy
Facilitator and service centre	Contact point, Conduit of information and technology	
	Training ground	Marketing, Production

Source: See text.

foreign investors. As has been mentioned before, such "window" companies include 72 official companies, 530 unofficial companies, and thousands of "agent windows".

From 1984 to 1986 Chinese companies acquired control of three Hong Kong listed companies in rescue operations, namely Conic Investment in 1984 and the Ka Wah and Union Banks in 1986. The Chinese strategy was then passive. From 1987 onwards China's strategy changed, and China made active use of Hong Kong's stock market to tap funds for Chinese enterprises. As new companies do not have the track record to meet the listing criteria of the Hong Kong stock exchange, Chinese companies acquire control of small Hong Kong listed companies and get de facto listings under the shell of the listed companies. In 1987 Guangdong Enterprise acquired Union Globe Development and assumed its listing (Ni 1994, p. 9). Many princeling companies also acquired control of small Hong Kong listed companies, and the prices of their shares usually rose greatly after acquisition, as connection with the Chinese leadership was perceived to be an important asset. For instance, after Deng Zifang acquired Kadar Investment, the price of its shares rose 30% in one day (*United Daily News*, Hong Kong, 20 May 1993).

In 1992 the three traditional giants among Chinese companies in Hong Kong, namely China Merchants, China Travel Service, and China Resources, reorganized themselves into holding companies and were listed on Hong Kong's stock exchange. The listings were very successful, and China Merchants' shares were oversubscribed 373 times, while China Travel Service's were oversubscribed 412 times, setting new records of oversubscription in the Hong Kong stock market. As has been mentioned before, Red Chips and H. Shares became an important component of the Hong Kong stock market. By May 1997 they constituted well over 10% of the capitalization of the Hong Kong stock market.

Hong Kong's share in China's foreign loans is substantial. According to Chinese statistics, from 1979 to 1996 China's utilized foreign loans from Hong Kong amounted to US$4.8 billion, or 4.6% of the total. Chinese statistics only include loans guaranteed by state agencies and exclude the bulk of loans extended to foreign-invested enterprises in China. Hong Kong's financial institutions, including the BOC Group, were important sources for the latter type of loan. The amount of such loans are available in Hong Kong banking statistics. In 1996 Hong Kong's net claims on non-bank customers in China amounted to US$7.6 billion. The share of the BOC Group in such loans is not known, but it is probably considerable.

Hong Kong plays a leading role in syndicating loans to China. Among China's commercial loans, 70% were syndicated loans, and over 60% were syndicated in Hong Kong (*Hong Kong Economic Journal Monthly*, Hong Kong, August, 1992) The BOC first participated in Hong Kong's international syndicated loan market in 1979 and has since regularly joined hands with multinational banks in syndicating loans to China.

Hong Kong as Trading Partner

This only refers to trade involving China and Hong Kong as final markets (i.e. Chinese goods consumed in Hong Kong and Hong Kong goods consumed in China). The much more extensive entrepôt trade is covered under the middleman function. As has been mentioned, though China has been unable to capture the higher end of Hong Kong's market, Hong Kong has still been consuming substantial amounts of Chinese exports. It consumed around US$5.7 billion worth in 1997, which amounts to 3.1% of China's exports or 7.6% of Hong Kong's retained imports (Table 1.7). The China Resource Company still has dominant market shares in live and fresh food, toilet tissue, polyester cotton cloth, and cotton grey cloth. Its markets shares in yarn, petroleum, cement, steel, and toy circuits are hefty (China Resources Group 1994, p. 47). Moreover, China has a vast trading and retail network in Hong Kong that was developed in the 1960s and 1970s. Given the change in taste in Hong Kong, Chinese department stores have survived by diversifying their source of consumer products, offering Japanese and European consumer products in addition to Chinese products. The China Resource Company also diversified its operations. Besides its twelve large department stores, it has established a chain of petrol stations and thirty-seven supermarkets. It has also diversified into banking, financing, energy, transportation, communications, building and construction, manufacturing, real estate, and tourism.

Service trade between China and Hong Kong has increased by leaps and bounds in the open-door era. As is mentioned in Chapter 4, China and Hong Kong have become each other's foremost source of tourist arrivals. It is not surprising that China Travel Service has expanded its operations tremendously, and other Chinese companies including China Resources, China Merchants, and Guangdong Enterprises have also diversified into tourism.

Hong Kong as Middleman

As is mentioned in Chapter 4, the decentralization of the Chinese system of foreign trade has enhanced the position of Hong Kong as

China's middleman, because decentralization increases the cost of searching for a suitable trading partner. The vast number of "window" companies and trading firms that China has established in Hong Kong have demonstrated that China recognizes the established efficiency of Hong Kong in trading.

As Hong Kong is the busiest container port in the world and the dominant transportation hub of China, it is hardly surprising that Chinese companies have invested heavily in Hong Kong's transportation sector. For instance, the China Resources Group, the China Merchants Group, China Travel Service, and Guangdong Enterprises have invested heavily in container terminals, shipping, air freight, aviation, and warehouses. Ni observes that "almost every mainland window company has diversified into transportation since 1985" (Ni 1994, p. 14).

Hong Kong as Service Centre and Facilitator

China values Hong Kong as a contact point with the world. Hong Kong is the major centre for China's trade and also the centre of consultancy services for businesspeople aiming at the China market. Most Chinese companies in Hong Kong, including the "window" companies, offer consultancy services.

The Chinese also value Hong Kong as a conduit of market information and technology transfer. China has established companies specializing in market information in Hong Kong, including the well-known Southeast Economic Information Centre. China's investment in Hong Kong manufacturing is often related to technology transfer. In 1985 China became the third-largest investor in Hong Kong manufacturing, after the United States and Japan. For instance, China has established two relatively high-technology electronics firms in Hong Kong that produce integrated circuits. The engineers in these firms come mostly from China, and the firms have attracted public attention because of an initial U.S. ban, later lifted, on supplying training and equipment to them (Sung 1991, p. 28). China also uses Hong Kong as a market testing ground to gauge consumer acceptance of its new products through its vast distribution network.

Given the economies of agglomeration in most services and Hong Kong's position as the service centre of China, it is hardly surprising that Chinese companies have invested so heavily in Hong Kong's service sector.

Political Determinants of Chinese Investment

Before the open-door era, political considerations were important in Chinese investment in Hong Kong. The Chinese Communist Party initially established businesses in Hong Kong to act as a cover and also to generate revenue for underground activities (Xu 1993, p. 244). Chinese companies run five newspapers in Hong Kong as part of China's propaganda effort, and they account for one-tenth of the newspaper circulation in Hong Kong. In support of China's propaganda effort, China has invested in publishing, book stores, magazines, news agencies, and motion picture production and distribution.

Maintaining Hong Kong's Prosperity during the Transition

Political factors are still important to Hong Kong / Mainland business relations. The 1997 crisis led to the exodus of British capital and Hong Kong Chinese capital. To maintain the prosperity of Hong Kong during its transition to Chinese sovereignty, Xu Jiatun's proposed strategy was "to lure British capital to stay, to stabilize Hong Kong Chinese capital, to promote foreign capital, to foster unity with overseas Chinese capital and Taiwanese capital, and to strengthen Chinese capital" (Xu 1993, p. 229). China has actively used its investment in Hong Kong as a vehicle to pursue its goals.

"To stabilize Hong Kong Chinese capital", the NCNA has on several occasions asked the BOC to extend loans to friendly Hong Kong magnates in financial crises. The better-known cases include the Hong Kong magnate Fung King Hey (Xu 1993, pp. 131–2), the Bank of East Asia (Xu 1993, p. 238), and C. Y. Tung, shipping magnate and father of Tung Chee-hwa, the first chief executive of the HKSAR (Hong Kong Special Administrative Region).

The BOC and the NCNA have repeatedly intervened to stabilize financial crises. In 1985 CITIC (Hong Kong) acquired the Ka Wah Bank to avert a crisis. In 1986 the China Merchants Group acquired the insolvent Union Bank. In October 1987, after the worldwide stock market crash, the Hang Seng Futures Exchange was insolvent. The Hong Kong government, the Hong Kong Bank, and the BOC mounted a joint rescue operation, and the BOC pledged a loan of HK$100 million. The decision process involved Zhao Ziyang, then the premier of China (Xu 1993, pp. 198–200). In 1991 there was a run on the Standard Chartered Bank due to rumours, and the crisis was averted after the Hong Kong Bank and the BOC jointly pledged their support.

Interpenetration of Economics and Politics

Since the signing of the Sino-British Declaration in 1984, there was a subtle interpenetration of economics and politics involving Chinese companies in Hong Kong. As insurance against the uncertainties of 1997, Hong Kong capital has sought allies overseas as well as in China. The courtship of Hong Kong magnates and princelings in joint-ventures has already been noted.

British capital has traditionally dominated the highly regulated sectors of the Hong Kong economy due to favouritism on the part of the colonial government. These sectors include public utilities, aviation, telecommunication, and banking. While banking has been progressively liberalized since the 1970s, the liberalization of the other sectors has just started. To protect their monopoly rents after 1997, these British companies have forged alliances with powerful Chinese companies. For instance, CITIC has purchased 25% of Cathay Pacific and 28.5% of Dragonair. Table 5.8 shows the extensive participation of influential Chinese companies in the regulated infrastructure sectors of Hong Kong. The rapid influx of Chinese capital into such sectors is likely to retard their liberalization, as Chinese firms are politically influential.

Table 5.8
Chinese Companies' Stake in the Infrastructure Sector of Hong Kong, 1997

Mainland Company	Hong Kong Company	Infrastructure Sector	% Share
CITIC /	Cathay Pacific	Aviation Services	25.00
CITIC Pacific	Eastern Harbour Tunnel	Sea Tunnel Services	25.00
	Western Harbour Tunnel	Sea Tunnel Services	35.00
	Dragonair	Aviation Services	28.50
	HACTL	Aviation Services	10.00
	China Light & Power	Power	20.00
CAAC	Jardine Air	Aviation Ground Services	40.00
	Dragonair	Aviation Services	35.86
China Telecom	Hong Kong Telecom	Telecom services	5.50
China Everbright	Hong Kong Telecom	Telecom services	7.70
China Resources	Modern Terminal	Container Harbour	10.00
	Tunnel Services	Tunnel Services	20.00
China Merchants	Modern Terminal	Container Harbour Services	13.00
COSCO	Container Terminal 8	Container Harbour Services	50.00
China Travel Service	City Bus	Bus	20.00

Note: Updated table based on Ni 1994, p. 13. (see note f, Table 5.4)

Future Trends

In the reform era, Hong Kong's investment in China appears to be substantially larger than the reverse flow. Hong Kong's cumulative direct investment in China amounted to US$99.3 billion at the end of 1996, exceeding China's US$14.8 billion investment in Hong Kong by a substantial margin. However, the estimate of Chinese investment in Hong Kong is likely to be biased downwards, as there is an incentive for China's local authorities and enterprises to establish unofficial subsidiaries in Hong Kong to evade controls on foreign trade and foreign exchange. Hong Kong's investment in China is significantly exaggerated, as it includes investment from the subsidiaries of other multinationals incorporated in Hong Kong. Moreover, officials in planned economies tend to exaggerate economic performance (the "success indicators" problem). Anecdotal evidence suggests that Hong Kong investors often overstate the value of their investments in China with the co-operation of local officials. For example, Hong Kong manufacturers tend to put a high value on the outdated machinery that they move to China.

As China continues to liberalize its foreign exchange controls, it is expected that more and more Chinese capital will flow to Hong Kong through official as well as unofficial channels. It is natural for Chinese enterprises and investors to move their capital to Hong Kong, as Hong Kong has stricter protection of property rights than China does, and the funds can also be used much more flexibly in Hong Kong. In the long run, Chinese investment in Hong Kong may rival Hong Kong's investment in China.

Notes

1. See section on "Subregional Economic Integration" in Chapter 2 for a more detailed account of the growth triangles.

2. The data on imports of raw materials and components used in processed exports are published in China Customs Statistics. It is thus possible to compute the processing margin. The estimation of Hong Kong's re-export margin is explained in Chapter 4.

3. For a detailed account of the various estimates of Chinese investment in Hong Kong, see Sung 1996, pp. 13–17.

4. Information obtained from interview.

CHAPTER 6

Trade and Investment Involving Taiwan

Taiwan's Investment in China

Despite the explosive growth of Taiwanese investment on the Mainland in recent years, the total stock of contracted Taiwanese investment in the Mainland at the end of 1996 was only 16% of that of Hong Kong (Table 2.5). This indicates considerable potential for further expansion of the Taiwanese share. However, the 1994 "Thousand Islands" incident[1] and China's hostility towards Lee Teng Hui in 1995 and 1996 slowed down Taiwan's investment in China.

Taiwan's investment had largely been in small-scale, labour-intensive operations producing light manufactured goods for export. The industries included textiles, shoes, umbrellas, travel accessories, and electronics, and were concentrated in Fujian (particularly Xiamen) and Guangdong. However, Taiwanese investment is increasing in scale and sophistication, with an increasing number of more technology-intensive projects such as chemicals, building materials, automobiles, and electronic products and components entering the picture. The fields of investment have diversified from manufacturing into real estate, finance, tourism, and agriculture. The location of investment has also spread inland from the coast.

The surge of Taiwanese investment in the Mainland raised fears that such investment would lead to the "hollowing out" of Taiwan industry and would pose a security threat. In July 1990 the Taiwan government tried to cool down the PRC investment boom by improving the investment environment in Taiwan and by steering investment away from the Mainland to ASEAN countries. Both carrots and sticks were used to prevent Formosa Plastics from implementing its gigantic project to build a naphtha cracking plant in Xiamen. To control the mainland investment boom, Taiwan does not allow investment in industries that are still competitive in Taiwan. However, business people have often been able to evade these controls.

Taiwan's president visited ASEAN countries in early 1994 in an effort to improve the investment environment for Taiwanese investors there. The Taiwanese government is attempting to guide the mainland investment boom rather than to reverse it. There are real political differences dividing the Mainland and Taiwan — differences that are not going to disappear soon. However, if Taiwan continues to liberalize its relations with the Mainland, Taiwanese investment in China will probably eventually rival that of Hong Kong.

Taiwan's Trade with China

Like Hong Kong's, Taiwan's investment in China has generated huge trade flows. The bulk of Taiwan's exports to China consist of raw materials, semi-manufactured goods, and machinery supplied to Taiwanese enterprises on the Mainland (Kao and Sung, 1995, p. 79). Semi-manufactured goods were not that important in the Mainland's exports to Taiwan because of Taiwan's restrictions on such imports in the past. However, the share of semi-manufactured goods is rising as a result of the liberalization of Taiwan's import controls.

Because of Taiwan's policy of no direct trade, Taiwan-Mainland trade is conducted via third ports, including Hong Kong, Okinawa, Pusan, Guam, and Singapore. Both Taiwan's and the Mainland's statistics on Taiwan–Mainland trade are biased downwards, because it is not possible to trace the final destination of exports and the true origin of imports through so many third ports.

As the bulk of Taiwan–Mainland trade goes through Hong Kong, which has detail statistics on the origin and destination of re-exports, Hong Kong statistics on re-exports of Taiwanese origin to China and vice versa have often been used by researchers to gauge the magnitude of Taiwan–Mainland trade. What is not well known is the existence of substantial "direct trade" between Taiwan and the Mainland.

As is mentioned in Chapter 3, this trade usually involves switching trade documents, because of Taiwan's ban on direct trade with the Mainland. Taiwanese exporters claim that their goods are destined for Hong Kong when the goods leave Taiwan. However, on arrival in Hong Kong, the documents are switched and the new documents claim that the goods are destined for the Mainland. As the goods are consigned to a buyer in the Mainland, they do not go through Hong Kong customs, and no Hong Kong firm can claim legal possession of the goods. Such goods are regarded as transshipment by the Hong Kong government and are not considered part of Hong Kong's trade. Such trade is considered "direct trade" in this book because no third party buys the goods involved for resale. By switching trade documents, the Taiwanese exporters save 0.1% of the cost of going through Hong Kong customs. This "direct trade" also has the advantage of confidentiality, because Hong Kong customs do not keep records of trade.

In terms of transportation, the "direct trade" between Taiwan and the Mainland takes three forms, namely transshipment, transit shipment, and illegal direct shipment. *Transshipment* involves the uploading and downloading of cargo from one vessel to another, usually in Hong Kong waters. As Taiwan does not permit regular shipping services between Taiwan and the Mainland, transshipment is the dominant mode of "direct trade". The Hong Kong government has statistics on the volume of transshipment by weight but not by value, since transshipped goods do not clear Hong Kong customs.

In October 1988 Taiwan allowed charted ships flying the flags of third countries to sail across the Taiwan Straits as long as they stopped in a third place on their voyage. Taiwanese businesses have chartered ships flying the flags of third countries to carry cargo across the Taiwanese straits without changing vessels. The ships usually stop in Hong Kong and are treated by the Hong Kong government as "cargo in transit". *Transit shipment* entails considerable savings in money as well as in time, as no downloading and uploading is involved. The Hong Kong government does not have statistics on cargo in transit.

Since the early 1990s Taiwan has accepted "switch bills" as indirect trade, partly because the government is quite powerless to stop the trade. However, the Taiwanese government stipulates that cargo in containers should change vessels in third ports (i.e., transshipment via third ports). For bulk cargo, transit shipment via third ports is accepted, and changing of vessels is not required because it is expensive and impractical. For example, Taiwanese businesspeople have complained that it is impractical to require changing of vessels for vessels containing kaolin, which sticks to the vessel.

It is known from press reports and interviews that *illegal direct shipment* involving chartered ships flying flags of third countries does exist. Though illegal direct shipment obviously saves transportation costs, it is risky, as shipping records are public information, and the Taiwan government can check whether the ship has passed through Hong Kong or a third port. There have been cases in which ships were fined for illegal direct shipment (Sung 1994, p. 14).

In the above three forms of "direct trade", Taiwan usually records the exports as destined for Hong Kong. However, the goods are not imported into Hong Kong, as they are shipped to the Mainland. Thus, Taiwan's "direct exports" to the Mainland can be estimated from Taiwan's "missing exports", which are equal to the difference between Taiwan's exports to Hong Kong and Hong Kong's imports from Taiwan after adjusting for the cost of insurance and freight (i.e., the difference between c.i.f. and f.o.b. prices). This is the trade-partners statistics technique. This differential is 1.63% for Hong Kong–Taiwan trade (Census and Statistics Department, 1998).

For Hong Kong's re-exports of Taiwanese goods, we have to take into account the re-export margin as well as the c.i.f. – f.o.b. differential. The re-export margin of Hong Kong re-exports of Taiwanese goods is taken to be 6%, which is the lowest figure on re-exports of non-Mainland origin (Table 4.1). The lowest figure is taken because Taiwanese goods have to go through Hong Kong by Taiwanese rules. Hong Kong traders may not perform much of a middleman role. Such exports are often handled by Taiwanese companies specifically established in Hong Kong for the purpose. Hong Kong's f.o.b. prices of its re-exports of Taiwanese goods are thus 7.7% higher than the f.o.b. prices of Taiwan's exports of such goods ($1.0163 \times 1.06 = 1.077$).

Table 6.1 shows the estimation of the value of Taiwan's "missing exports" to Hong Kong. The trade flows are converted to Taiwan's f.o.b. prices. From 1975 to 1988, Hong Kong's imports from Taiwan were more or less the same as Taiwan's exports to Hong Kong. Since 1989 Taiwan's exports to Hong Kong have exceeded Hong Kong's imports from Taiwan (converted to Taiwan's f.o.b. prices) by an increasingly large margin.

Taiwan's Exports to the Mainland

Table 6.2 shows Taiwan's direct and indirect trade with Mainland. Taiwan's "direct exports" to Mainland are taken to be Taiwan's "missing exports" to Hong Kong. In 1997 Taiwan's total exports to the Mainland were valued at US$21.9 billion (18.5% of Taiwan's exports), composed of US$12.9 billion of "direct" exports and US$9.1 billion of indirect exports.

In 1992 the Mainland surpassed Japan to become Taiwan's second-largest market (after the United States). In 1996, the market shares of Taiwan's top four markets (the United States, China, Japan, and Hong Kong) in Taiwan's exports were 24.2%, 18.5%, 9.6%, and 4.8% (excluding re-exports), respectively. Hong Kong's market share would be 23.5% if exports via Hong Kong to Mainland and elsewhere were included. Hong Kong may soon become

Table 6.1

Taiwan's Exports to Hong Kong and the Mainland, 1988–96

(US$ million)

			Taiwan's Exports to Hong Kong				China's Imports from Taiwan
			Imported into Hong Kong				
			Retained for Internal Use	Re-exported		Missing Exports	
	Total	Subtotal		to China	Else-where		
1988	5,580 (100)	5,600 (100.4)	3,320 (59.5)	2,097 (37.6)	183 (3.3)	—	—
1989	7,030 (100)	6,538 (93.0)	3,483 (49.5)	2,712 (38.6)	343 (4.9)	492 (7.0)	1,856
1990	8,570 (100)	7,377 (86.1)	3,946 (46.0)	3,070 (35.8)	361 (4.2)	1,193 (13.9)	2,254
1991	12,418 (100)	9,487 (76.4)	4,506 (36.3)	4,350 (35.0)	631 (5.1)	2,931 (23.6)	3,639
1992	15,427 (100)	11,106 (72.0)	4,577 (29.7)	5,882 (38.1)	647 (4.2)	4,321 (28.0)	5,881
1993	18,455 (100)	11,991 (65.0)	4,296 (23.3)	7,043 (38.2)	652 (3.5)	6,464 (35.0)	12,933
1994	21,263 (100)	13,671 (64.3)	5,053 (23.8)	7,983 (37.5)	635 (3.0)	7,592 (35.7)	14,085
1995	26,123 (100)	16,363 (62.6)	6,353 (24.3)	9,260 (35.5)	750 (2.9)	9,760 (37.4)	14,784
1996	26,788 (100)	15,628 (58.3)	5,762 (21.5)	9,100 (34.0)	766 (2.9)	11,160 (41.7)	16,182
1997	28,708 (100)	15,831 (55.1)	5,836 (20.3)	9,088 (31.7)	907 (3.2)	12,877 (44.9)	16,442

Sources: Data for Taiwan's exports to Hong Kong come from the *Monthly Bulletin of Statistics of the Republic of China*, Directorate-General of Budget, Accounting and Statistics, Executive Yuan, Republic of China; the amount imported into Hong Kong are taken to be Hong Kong's imports from Taiwan (obtained from *Hong Kong Review of Overseas Trade*, Census and Statistics Department, Hong Kong) less a 1.6% margin to allow for the cost of freight and insurance. Taiwan's exports re-exported via Hong Kong to China and elsewhere are taken to be Hong Kong's re-export of Taiwanese goods to China and elsewhere (obtained from *Hong Kong Review of Overseas Trade*) less a 7.7% margin to allow for the re-export mark-up and the cost of insurance and freight. Taiwan's re-exports retained for internal use in Hong Kong is obtained as a residual. "Direct exports" to China is also obtained as a residual. Data for China's imports from Taiwan come from *China Customs Statistics*, Economic Information & Agency, Hong Kong.

Note: Figures in brackets represent the row percentage distribution of Taiwan's exports to HK.

Table 6.2

Taiwan's "Direct" and Indirect Trade with the Mainland, 1986–97

	Exports (US$ million)			Imports (US $million)			Transshipment via Hong Kong (ton)	
	"Direct"	Indirect[a]	Total	"Direct"	Indirect[b]	Total	To China	From China
1986	–	753 (1.9)	753 (1.9)	–	146 (0.6)	146 (0.6)	1,392	800
1987	–	1,021 (1.9)	1,021 (1.9)	–	293 (0.8)	293 (0.8)	1,912	900
1988	–	2,097 (3.5)	2,097 (3.5)	–	486 (1.0)	486 (1.0)	8,096	2,595
1989	492 (0.7)	2,712 (4.1)	3,204 (4.8)	96 (0.2)	596 (1.1)	692 (1.3)	53,450	6,662
1990	1,193 (1.8)	3,070 (4.6)	4,263 (6.4)	328 (0.6)	778 (1.4)	1,106 (2.0)	81,195	12,447
1991	2,931 (3.9)	4,350 (5.7)	7,281 (9.6)	611 (1.0)	1,149 (1.8)	1,760 (2.8)	345,700	87,610
1992	4,321 (5.3)	5,882 (7.2)	10,203 (12.5)	716 (1.0)	1,146 (1.6)	1,862 (2.6)	872,292	211,026
1993	6,464 (7.6)	7,043 (8.3)	13,507 (15.9)	1,090 (1.4)	1,122 (1.5)	2,212 (2.9)	1,152,363	329,548
1994	7,592 (8.2)	7,983 (8.6)	15,575 (16.8)	1,579 (1.9)	1,317 (1.5)	2,896 (3.4)	1,227,000	442,000
1995	9,760 (8.7)	9,260 (8.3)	19,020 (17.0)	2,082 (2.0)	1,604 (1.6)	3,686 (3.6)	1,718,000	557,000
1996	11,160 (9.6)	9,100 (7.9)	20,260 (17.5)	2,392 (2.3)	1,622 (1.6)	4,014 (3.9)	1,988,000	626,000
1997	12,877 (10.6)	9,088 (7.9)	21,965 (18.5)	2,913 (2.5)	1,785 (1.6)	4,698 (4.1)	2,453,000	758,000

Sources: Data on indirect trade: *Annual Review of Hong Kong External Trade*, Census and Statistics Department, Hong Kong, various issues. "Direct trade": See text. Transshipment: *Hong Kong Shipping Statistics*, Census and Statistics Department, Hong Kong, various issues.

Note: Figures in brackets represent percentage share of Taiwan's total exports and imports. ton = tonnes.
   (a) Taiwan's indirect exports are taken to be Hong Kong's re-exports to China of Taiwan origin less a 7.7% margin to allow for the re-export mark-up and the cost of insurance and freight.
   (b) Taiwan's indirect imports are taken to be Hong Kong's re-exports to Taiwan of China origin plus a 1.6% margin to allow for the cost of insurance and freight.

Taiwan's largest market if we include Taiwan's exports via Hong Kong to Mainland and also to third countries in our calculations.

The estimation of the commodity composition of "direct exports" using the trade-partner statistics technique may not be reliable, as the commodity classification of Taiwan and the Mainland may not be consistent. However, it is possible to gauge the commodity composition of Taiwan's exports to the Mainland using China's import statistics. China's recorded 1996 imports from Taiwan were US$16.2 billion, which includes the bulk of Taiwan's exports to China.

The main commodities imported by the Mainland from Taiwan in 1996 were: machinery and mechanical appliances (22.4%), plastics (14.4%), electrical machinery and equipment (12.9%), and man-made filaments (6.9%). Not surprisingly, these were related to Taiwan's investment in China.

Taiwan's Imports from the Mainland

Unlike its exports, Taiwan's imports from the Mainland are restricted to selected commodity categories. Prohibited mainland goods are imported into Taiwan with fake country-of-origin certificates, which can be obtained in Thailand, for example, for a mere US$100. Thus, we cannot assume that Taiwan's "direct imports" from the Mainland are the difference between Taiwan's imports from Hong Kong and Hong Kong's exports to Taiwan, since Taiwan's "direct imports" from the Mainland are recorded as imports from Thailand or other countries where fake country-of-origin certificates are obtainable.

As is shown in Table 6.2, figures for Taiwan's "direct imports" from China before 1993 were obtained from figures for China's exports to Taiwan (converted to Taiwan's c.i.f. prices) as recorded in *China Customs Statistics*. However, China's statistics vastly overstate China's "direct exports" to Taiwan since 1993 as a result of the reclassification in that year to include China's indirect exports via Hong Kong. Taiwan's "direct imports" since 1993 were estimated from the value of the weight of Hong Kong's transshipment of mainland goods to Taiwan and an estimate of the value per ton of such transshipment. The latter is obtained from 1992 data (dividing Taiwan's 1992 "direct imports" by the weight of transshipment), and then adjusted for inflation using the unit value index of Hong Kong's imports from China. This gives an estimate of "direct imports" valued at US$2.9 billion in 1997, which exceeds the US$1.8 billion value of indirect imports in that year by a large margin. Between 1991 and 1993 Hong Kong re-exports of mainland goods to Taiwan stagnated, while transshipment of mainland goods to Taiwan continued to soar (Table 6.2). There was evidently a substitution of "direct" for indirect trade.

Taiwan's imports from the Mainland are much less significant than imports going the other direction, but the rate of growth of the former has been very high. In 1997 mainland products accounted for 4.1% of Taiwan's imports, and the Mainland was the sixth-largest supplier of Taiwan, after Japan (25.4%), the United States (20.3%), Germany (4.7%), and South Korea (4.3%), and France (4.1%).

Though the commodity composition of Taiwan's imports from the Mainland is difficult to estimate, it can be gauged from Mainland's exports to Taiwan, which were valued at US$ 2.8 billion in 1996, covering the bulk of Taiwan's import from China. The major commodities in 1996 were as follows: electrical machinery and equipment (16.9%), machinery and mechanical appliances (9%), iron and steel (7.4%), mineral oils and products (6.9%), and clothing (5%). There is substantial intra-industry trade across the Taiwan Straits, and this is one indication that the trade is investment related.

Taiwan has a massive surplus in its commodity trade with the Mainland, partly because of Taiwan's policy of only importing selective commodity items from the Mainland and partly because of China's lack of competitiveness in producing items demanded in Taiwan. However, Taiwan has large deficits with the Mainland in tourism, gifts and remittances, and investment. The payments balance across the Taiwan Strait is thus more even. Moreover,

Chapter 6

Table 6.3
The Mainland's "Direct" and Indirect Trade with Taiwan, 1986–96
(US$ million)

	Imports			Exports		
	"Direct"	Indirect	Total	"Direct"	Indirect	Total
1986	–	819 (1.9)	819 (1.9)	–	126 (0.4)	126 (0.4)
1987	–	1,111 (2.6)	1,111 (2.6)	–	253 (0.6)	253 (0.6)
1988	–	2,282 (4.1)	2,282 (4.1)	–	419 (0.9)	419 (0.9)
1989	505 (0.9)	2,951 (5.0)	3,456 (5.9)	94 (0.2)	514 (1.0)	608 (1.2)
1990	1,225 (2.3)	3,340 (6.3)	4,565 (8.6)	320 (0.5)	671 (1.1)	991 (1.6)
1991	3,009 (4.7)	4,733 (7.4)	7,742 (12.1)	595 (0.8)	991 (1.4)	1,586 (2.2)
1992	4,436 (5.7)	6,400 (8.2)	10,836 (13.9)	698 (0.8)	988 (1.2)	1,686 (2.0)
1993	6,635 (6.4)	7,663 (7.4)	14,298 (13.8)	1,062 (1.2)	967 (1.1)	2,029 (2.3)
1994	7,793 (6.7)	8,686 (7.5)	16,479 (14.2)	1,538 (1.3)	1,135 (0.9)	2,673 (2.2)
1995	10,019 (7.6)	10,075 (7.6)	20,094 (15.2)	2,028 (1.4)	1,383 (0.9)	3,411 (2.3)
1996	11,456 (8.2)	9,901 (7.1)	21,357 (15.4)	2,330 (1.5)	1,398 (0.9)	3,728 (2.4)
1997	13,218 (9.3)	9,888 (6.9)	23,106 (16.2)	2,838 (1.6)	1,539 (0.8)	4,377 (2.4)

Source: Estimated from Table 6.2 by adjusting for c.i.f. and f.o.b. price differences:
China's "direct" imports equal 1.0265[a] times Taiwan's "direct" exports.
China's indirect imports equal 1.088[b] times Taiwan's indirect exports.
China's "direct" exports equal Taiwan's "direct" imports divided by 1.0265[a].
China's indirect exports equal Taiwan's indirect imports divided by 1.16[c].

Notes: Figures in brackets represent percentage share of China total exports and imports.

(a) The f.o.b. – c.i.f. margin for Hong Kong–Mainland trade is 1%. The total margin for "direct" trade is thus 1.0163 (margin for Hong Kong–Taiwan trade) x 1.01 = 1.0265

(b) The total margin for indirect imports is 1.0265 (margin for "direct" trade) x 1.06 (re-exports margin of Taiwanese goods) = 1.088

(c) The total margin for indirect exports is 1.0265 (margin for "direct" trade) x 1.13 (re-export margin of mainland goods) = 1.16

intra-industry trade is expected to develop rapidly with the surge of Taiwanese investment on the Mainland and the further liberalization of Taiwan's controls on imports from the Mainland.

Mainland's Commodity Trade with Taiwan

Table 6.3 supplies figures for Mainland's "direct" and indirect trade with Taiwan. The numbers are obtained from Table 6.2 by adjusting for the difference in f.o.b. and c.i.f. prices, which can be substantial because of complications in the shipping arrangements and also because of the re-export margin earned by Hong Kong traders.

By 1991 Mainland's imports from Taiwan constituted 12.1% of its total imports, and Taiwan surpassed Hong Kong and the United States to become the Mainland's second-largest supplier (after Japan). In 1997 the shares of Japan and Taiwan in China's imports were 20.4% and 16.2%, respectively. Taiwan also became a significant market for the Mainland, accounting for 2.4% of China's exports (Table 6.3).

Service Trade between China and Taiwan

Service trade between China and Taiwan is largely restricted to Taiwanese tourists visiting China. Taiwan is the third-largest source of tourists into China, accounting for 2.8% of tourist arrivals there in 1996. The Taiwanese share of tourist expenditures in China is likely to be a few times higher than its share in tourist arrivals because, on a per capita basis, the Taiwanese visitor spends much more than do short-term visitors from Hong Kong and Macao. Most Taiwanese visiting China do so via Hong Kong. While Taiwan was among the leading sources of tourists to Hong Kong from 1988 to 1993, 1.5 million of the 1.75 million Taiwanese tourists visiting Hong Kong in 1993 went to the Mainland (*Hong Kong Economic Journal*, Hong Kong, 13 April 1994).

Trade and Investment between Hong Kong and Taiwan

Before 1987 economic ties between Hong Kong and Taiwan were one-sided because of Taiwan's trade protectionism and foreign exchange controls. The Hong Kong market was open to Taiwan, Hong Kong investors were free to invest in Taiwan, and Hong Kong tourists were free to go there, but movements in the opposite direction were restricted. In the mid 1970s Hong Kong became Taiwan's third-largest market (after the United States and Japan), accounting for roughly 7% of Taiwan's exports. However, Hong Kong exports to Taiwan were minimal as a result of Taiwan's barriers. Since the 1950s Hong Kong has been the third-largest investor in Taiwan, after the United States and Japan, but Taiwanese investment in Hong Kong was insignificant. Since the 1960s Taiwan has become an important destination for Hong Kong tourists, but few Taiwanese tourists visited Hong Kong as a result of Taiwan's controls on foreign exchange and departures.

However, economic ties developed rapidly in the late 1980s with the liberalization of Taiwan's import and foreign exchange controls, the sharp appreciation of Taiwanese currency, and Taiwan's use of Hong Kong as an intermediary in its interactions with China. Many Taiwanese toured Hong Kong on their way to the Mainland, with Taiwan becoming the foremost source of tourists for Hong Kong from 1988 to 1993[2] (20% of tourists arrivals in 1993). Taiwan also became a significant investor in Hong Kong. The share of the Taiwan market in Hong Kong's domestic exports jumped from 1% in 1985 to 3.3% in 1997, amounting to US$908 million. Since 1986 Taiwan has been the seventh-largest market for Hong Kong (after China, the United States, Singapore, Germany, Japan, and the United Kingdom).

In the 1990s Hong Kong was the fourth market for Taiwan, after the United States, China, and Japan. Taiwan's 1997 exports retained for internal use in Hong Kong were valued at US$5.8 billion and made up 4.8% of Taiwan's exports or 7.8% of the total retained imports of Hong Kong (Table 1.7). Taiwan is the third-largest supplier of Hong Kong's retained imports, after Japan and the United States.

Hong Kong investment in Taiwan has risen rapidly since the late 1980s. By the end of 1989 Hong Kong investment in Taiwan totalled US$1.2 billion (11% of total inward investment in Taiwan), while U.S. and Japanese investments were US$3 billion and US$2.9 billion, respectively. Hong Kong's cumulative investment in Taiwan rose to US$1.6 billion by the end of 1991 (Hong Kong Trade Development Council, 1992, p. 4), and US$2.5 billion (or 16% of total inward investment in Taiwan) by the end of 1995 (Table 1.3).

Taiwanese investment in Hong Kong also soared. According to Taiwan's statistics, Taiwan's outward FDI in Hong Kong amounted to US$604 million by the end of 1994. Taiwan's statistics on outward FDI are usually underestimates because firms may under report their outward FDI to evade Taiwan's foreign exchange controls. For instance, Taiwanese FDI in the Mainland as reported by mainland sources was 2.5 times that recorded by Taiwanese authorities. However, in the case of Taiwanese investment in Hong Kong, Taiwanese firms may misclassify their investments in the Mainland as investments in Hong Kong. We cannot be sure that US$604 million is an underestimate. According to recent Hong Kong government surveys on external investment, Hong Kong's average stock of inward FDI from Taiwan in 1996 was US$533 million. This is close to the Taiwanese figure.

As usual, press reports that 1995 cumulative investment from Taiwan amounted to US$4 billion or US$5 billion (*Hong Kong Daily News*, 8 August 1996) appear to be an exaggeration. Press reports may be based on asset value, which is normally a few times that of cumulative FDI. However, press report on the sectoral composition of Taiwanese investment in Hong Kong may be quite accurate, i.e., services accounted for over half of the investment, and export–import trade accounted for over 20%. The rest was accounted for mainly by finance and insurance.

The Future of Hong Kong–Taiwan Relations

After the reversion of Hong Kong to China, China's strategy has been to use the HKSAR as an example with which to woo Taiwan back to the fold. Taiwan has fears that its links with Hong Kong will be used against its interests by the Mainland. After 1 July 1997, in terms of visiting, residing, and investing in Taiwan, Hong Kong residents have had fewer rights than they did before, because they are now regarded as foreigners rather than as overseas Chinese.

The net effect of Hong Kong's reversion is the strengthening of Hong Kong–Taiwan relations. The lack of trust between China and Britain meant that the colonial government in Hong Kong had to keep Taiwanese officials at arm's length for fear for provoking China. The HKSAR Government can be more proactive *vis à vis* Taiwan.

Tung Chee-hwa, first chief executive of the HKSAR, is well connected with Taiwan. His sister is married to a former high-ranking official in Taiwan, and his family business had good connections with Taiwan. He has appointed Paul Yip, his political adviser, to handle Taiwan affairs. This shows that Tung considers Hong Kong–Taiwan relations to be of high priority.

Closer Hong Kong–Taiwan ties have been reflected in simplification of visa requirements. Starting April, 1998, Taiwan speeded up the processing of visas for Hong Kong residents from two weeks to one week. Multiple entry visas, valid for three years, were granted for frequent travellers. Starting June, 1998, Hong Kong speeded up the processing of multiple entry visas (valid for three years) for Taiwan residents from five days to two days. Moreover, Taiwan residents who have already obtained visas to enter the Mainland can stay in Hong Kong for 7 days without a Hong Kong visa when they enter (leave) the Mainland from (to) Hong Kong. Hong Kong announced the above measures in May 1998, as part of a package to stimulate the economy suffering from the East Asian financial crisis.

Notes

1. In 1994, a group of Taiwanese tourists were murdered on a ship at the Thousand Island resort in Zhejiang Province. Connivance of local authorities was suspected and there was widespread protests in Taiwan over China's handling of the case.

2. The Mainland has replaced Taiwan as the foremost source of tourists for Hong Kong from 1994 to 1996, partly due to the surge of visitors from the Mainland to Hong Kong, and partly due to the drop to Taiwanese tourists as a result of the "Thousand Island" incident and hostilities over the Taiwan Straits in 1995 and 1996.

CHAPTER 7

Policy Issues

This chapter will discuss the following three policy issues concerning the integration of Hong Kong and South China:

1. Formation of a South China trading bloc or an institution of tariff preferences.
2. Establishment of bonded areas, especially the creation of an industrial park at the Hong Kong–Shenzhen border.
3. Co-ordination of infrastructure developments between Hong Kong and South China.

A Greater China Trading Bloc?

As noted in Chapter 3, there is an obvious lack of institutional integration among the trio (the Mainland, Hong Kong, Taiwan). There have been many proposals to establish a trading bloc of Greater China, or of Greater South China, or of Greater Hong Kong (see p.1 and the map). These proposals are unrealistic and counter-productive.

The political differences between Taiwan and the Mainland are deep-seated, and it is not realistic to assume that a trading bloc including Greater China and involving Taiwan could be established. A trading bloc consisting of Hong Kong and the Mainland is also impractical.

Hong Kong has always been a free port, and the freedom of movement of goods and capital in Hong Kong is enshrined in the Sino-British agreement on the future of Hong Kong and in the Basic Law. All parties involved recognize that such freedom is essential to the future prosperity of Hong Kong. Hong Kong and the Mainland cannot form a customs union, for this requires a common external tariff. As the free-port status of Hong Kong is guaranteed by the Basic Law and by an international agreement, the only way the Mainland and Hong Kong could form a customs union would be for the Mainland to abolish all its tariffs. It is ridiculous to think that this could happen. No big country has ever abolished all its tariffs. The alternative is for Hong Kong to abandon its free-port status, which not only would violate the Basic Law but would also jeopardize Hong Kong's role as China's entrepôt.

Forming a common market of or an economic union between Hong Kong and the Mainland would violate more sections of the Basic Law. A common market would imply that Hong Kong would have to give up regulating migration from China. If this were to happen, Hong Kong would immediately face unmanageable population pressure. An economic union would imply that China would have to abolish all its foreign exchange and capital controls, as the Basic Law stipulates that Hong Kong will have complete freedom of capital movement.

It should be noted that it would be also be impractical for Hong Kong and the Mainland to form a Free Trade Area (FTA), which is the trade bloc with the lowest degree of formal economic integration. A FTA would not violate the Basic Law and would be beneficial to Hong Kong, as Hong Kong goods would be exempt from Chinese tariffs. However, the Mainland's exports to Hong Kong would not increase, because Hong Kong is already a free port. Moreover, the Mainland would lose some tariff revenue. Such an FTA is unlikely to be a win-win proposition and is thus impractical.

A South China Trading Bloc?

A Hong Kong–Guangdong trading bloc would be even more problematic than the propositions just mentioned, as it would imply the building of a fence separating Guangdong from the rest of China. Otherwise, Guangdong could not have different tariffs from the rest of the Mainland.

The idea that a customs union involving Hong Kong and Shenzhen could be formed is also unrealistic. Shenzhen has built a "second line" separating itself from the rest of China, and it has plans of becoming a free trade zone. Even if Shenzhen becomes a free trade zone, Hong Kong and Shenzhen will still be separate entities in trade. Trade between Hong Kong and Shenzhen will be similar to trade between Hong Kong and any other free trade zone, such as Singapore. Theoretically, Hong Kong and Shenzhen could enter the WTO as a single customs territory. The two regions would then have to bargain as a single entity in world trade and would also have to agree on the sharing of textile and clothing quotas. A prerequisite for that is Shenzhen's autonomy in external economic affairs. This implies that Beijing would relinquish control of Shenzhen's external economic affairs. China would also have to enter the WTO as the Mainland less Shenzhen, because Shenzhen's bargaining position in world trade may differ from that of Beijing. Another problem is that the union would undermine Hong Kong's autonomy. Hong Kong's freedom in external economic affairs is guaranteed by both the Sino-British agreement and the Basic Law, and Hong Kong is a member of the WTO. A trading bloc of Shenzhen and Hong Kong would give Beijing an institutional channel by which to encroach on Hong Kong's autonomy. Hong Kong has the largest clothing quota in the world and does not want to share it.

In the case that Shenzhen becomes a free trade zone, Hong Kong and Shenzhen would have to maintain their border controls against each other. To qualify for WTO membership, Hong Kong must be able to effectively distinguish between goods made in Hong Kong and those made in Shenzhen and elsewhere. The abolition of Hong Kong border controls against Shenzhen would jeopardize Hong Kong's WTO membership and Hong Kong's textile and clothing quotas. As China is applying for WTO membership, the abolition of Shenzhen's border controls against Hong Kong goods would also pose complications for China's WTO membership. Moreover, Hong Kong and Shenzhen have different import prohibitions. For example, Shenzhen cannot allow the free importation of political or religious literature from Hong Kong. The present controls governing the movement of people between Hong Kong and Shenzhen would also remain in effect. Hong Kong maintains strict controls on immigration from the Mainland due to overcrowding in Hong Kong. The need for such controls is recognized by both the Sino-British agreement and the Basic Law, and it is unlikely that Hong Kong will exempt Shenzhen from these controls. The immigration formalities for Hong Kong residents entering Shenzhen are very simple, and it is unlikely that the procedure could be further simplified. Shenzhen needs to maintain some controls on the entry of Hong Kong residents to prevent those it identifies as undesirable from entering the country. For example, during the riot in Shenzhen in August 1992, Shenzhen forbade the entry of Hong Kong reporters. Even if Shenzhen becomes a free trade zone, the present immigration and customs formalities for people and goods are unlikely to be simplified significantly.

Though the proposal of forming a South China trading bloc is unrealistic, the spontaneous and market-driven economic integration of Hong Kong, the Mainland, and Taiwan are proceeding rapidly. The foremost barrier to the economic integration of South China is the command economy of China, not its tariffs. In a command economy, administrative and quantitative import controls and foreign exchange controls are often so stringent that the resulting import premia are much higher than tariffs are. In such a case, unless the command economy is transformed into a market economy, tariff reduction will not do much to promote economic integration. Even in market economies, tariff preferences and institutional arrangements may not be important for economic integration. Economic integration means the lowering of transaction costs, and tariffs are often only a small part of transaction costs. Other factors such as transportation costs, cultural affinity, foreign exchange controls, and government regulations may be much more important. Integration in South China will proceed rapidly if China continues to uphold its open policy.

Measures to facilitate border crossings between Hong Kong and Shenzhen will enhance integration. Presently, businesspeople often complain about the congestion at the checkpoints along the border. It is worth considering issuance of special passes and passages for businesspeople who commute regularly between Hong Kong and Shenzhen. The proposal to provide round-the-clock customs service should also be implemented.

Tariff Preferences

Hong Kong businesspeople have repeatedly lobbied for tariff preferences from the Mainland. Such preferences, if granted, would be detrimental not only to the Mainland but also to Hong Kong. Free competition has long been the source of the strength and dynamism of the Hong Kong economy. Such preferences would entice Hong Kong businesspeople to spend their energy lobbying for favouritism instead of concentrating their resources on improving productivity. Moreover, there is no free lunch, and Hong Kong's seeking favouritism from the Mainland would invite the Mainland to ask for reciprocal favouritism from Hong Kong. Given the large number of mainland enterprises in Hong Kong, the pressure to indulge in favouritism is very strong. It should be stressed that the erosion of Hong Kong's autonomy and dynamism would also be detrimental to China's long-term interests.

It should be noted that Hong Kong and Taiwanese businesspeople already have a tremendous advantage in the mainland market because of geographic proximity and cultural affinity. If they cannot compete against foreigners in the mainland market, they must be highly inefficient, and they deserve to lose.

In June 1980 the Mainland abolished tariffs on Taiwanese products on the grounds that Taiwan is part of China. This policy predictably led to Hong Kong businesspeople's demands that they be given the same treatment. The Mainland's unilateral tariff preferences for Taiwan are "unGATTable", economically inefficient, and politically counter-productive. Both Taiwan and Hong Kong are Chinese territories. However, Taiwan receives special concessions that are denied to Hong Kong. Taiwanese businesspeople would conclude that this is because Taiwan's reunification with the

Mainland is not assured, while Hong Kong has already returned to the Mainland. To keep their concessions, Taiwanese businesspeople would have to maintain their separation from the Mainland. Surprisingly, this policy runs contrary to the goal of national reunification.

The Mainland's tariff exemption for Taiwan was short-lived. In June 1981 Beijing levied "adjustment taxes" on Taiwanese goods to stem the flood in the mainland market of Taiwanese goods and Hong Kong goods with fake Taiwanese certificate of origin. To save face, the adjustment taxes were slightly lower than the tariffs were. The episode illustrated the economic and political dangers of favouritism and discrimination.

However, Beijing has yet to learn the lesson completely. Special concessions were given to Taiwanese investors in 1989, and Beijing then had problems with investors putting on a Taiwanese disguise. There were also complaints of unfair competition from domestic producers in the Mainland whose exports have been displaced by the exports of Taiwanese investors in the Mainland.

Under the new 1991 joint-venture law, many concessions for Taiwanese investors were also given to other foreign investors. Beijing is prepared to abolish all special favours for Taiwanese to enter the WTO.

The best principle for handling the economic relations among Hong Kong, Taiwan, and the Mainland is non-discrimination and non-favouritism. Under this principle, market forces will be given full play. The entry of the Mainland and Taiwan into the WTO would promote the integration of South China in many ways. The principle of the WTO is non-discrimination. To qualify for GATT membership, the Mainland must radically reform its trading system, and Taiwan has to further liberalize its trade. This would create a greater scope in which market forces could strengthen the integration process. WTO membership would offer some recourse against protectionism and strengthen China's MFN status in the United States. This would reinforce the Mainland's open policy and would also strengthen Taiwan's international position. Taipei could thus afford to allow its ties with the Mainland to become better established.

Though Hong Kong, Taiwan, and the Mainland should not establish a formal trade bloc, the three can promote exchanges through consultation. With the implementation of the Uruguay Round starting in 1994, the MFA (Multi-fibre Arrangement) would be phased out in ten years. As the four members of the China Circle are major textile exporters and are also members of the MFA, their weight in textile negotiations is significant, and policy co-ordination among the four on the phasing out of the MFA should be explored. The traditional wisdom is that the MFA protects high-cost producers like Hong Kong or Taiwan at the expense of low-cost producers like the Mainland. Were it not for the MFA quotas, exports from low-cost producers would be free to expand at the expense of the market shares of the high-cost producers. This implies that Hong Kong and Taiwan should favour a slow phasing out of the MFA, whereas China should support the opposite. However, both Hong Kong and Taiwan have invested heavily in the textile and clothing industries in the Mainland. The interests of Hong Kong, Taiwan, and the Mainland on the phasing out of the MFA may thus be similar.

Bonded Areas

After Deng's 1992 southern tour, China established thirteen bonded areas along the coast. Three of the areas are in the Pearl River Delta, namely Guangzhou and Shenzhen's Futian and Sha-toujiao. Moreover, Shenzhen plans to "open up the first line (the Shenzhen–Hong Kong boundary), and tighten up the second line (boundary separating Shenzhen from China)", thus transforming Shenzhen into a huge bonded area.

Besides bonded areas, there are also many bonded warehouses and bonded factories in the Pearl River Delta. Products imported into bonded areas, warehouses, or factories are temporarily exempt from tariffs. Such goods are not assessed with tariffs if they are later exported. However, if they are imported into the country, then full tariffs will be levied.

A bonded area faces international prices and is an area of free trade, because no tariffs are levied. Bonded warehouses, factories, or areas are good for developing processed exports because imports for processing and re-exports are exempt from tariffs. Bonded areas are also good for developing the ancillary services of export processing, namely storage, transportation, and packaging.

In non-communist developing countries, tariffs are usually the main factor distorting the functioning of the economy, and bonded areas would eliminate this distortion. In China's traditional command economy, administrative intervention is the main distortion, and tariffs are of secondary importance. China's open policy thus started with the creation of SEZs that are exempt from many controls of the plan. By the early 1990s a nascent market economy had developed in the coastal open areas, and the establishment of bonded areas is the next logical step. The establishment of bonded areas is a sign of the maturation of the open policy. Bonded areas will also help China develop its backward service sector.

China's bonded areas are completely enclosed to present smuggling and to facilitate management. Workers pass through checkpoints to work inside them. There are no residents inside these areas. The arrangement minimizes the need to import consumer durables for use within the area and thus minimizes the loss in tariff revenue.

The Futian Bonded Area

Among the many bonded areas of China, Shenzhen's Futian has great potential because it is adjacent to Hong Kong. The Futian zone is connected to Hong Kong by the Lok Ma Chau bridge, and there is no need to pass through the customs of Shenzhen to travel between the two places. Futian is no more than a one-hour drive from most parts of Hong Kong, and foreigners can apply for a visa upon entry. Futian is intended to be a convenient place for Chinese and foreigners to make contact. It is expected that it will develop into a service centre specializing in international trade, exhibitions, information, finance, and insurance.

There are many other bonded areas in China whose goals are similar. The most notable among them is the Weigaoqiao bonded area in Shanghai, which has its own port. It is intended to be a hub of commerce and trade.

However, the development of both Futian and Weigaoqiao has failed to live up to the expectations of the planners. This is largely attributable to poor strategy. International experience shows that while bonded areas are good for export processing and storage, they are not suited to trading, finance, and related services. Many Chinese planners have the mistaken notion that the tariff-free status of bonded areas is important for the development of entrepôt trade. However, the location for negotiation of deals and processing of trade documents can be conducted quite far away from where goods are stored. For instance, many deals concluded in Hong Kong involve trade that does not touch Hong Kong at all. Negotiation on deals and processing of trade documents usually take place in a trading and business centre because of the economies of agglomeration mentioned in Chapter 4. Bonded areas, which are usually far away from the city centre to ensure that the area can be easily fenced in, are good for storage or export processing rather than for service activities.

The other problem with bonded areas in China is that local governments want to use them as another excuse to give special tax breaks to attract foreign investment. While special tax breaks had a role in the initial stage of the open policy, a mature investment environment should not need to rely on them. Moreover, China is preparing to enter the WTO, which requires uniform or national treatment for all, and it will be phasing out the special tax breaks for SEZs and foreign investors. However, the competition for foreign investment among localities in China is very keen, and local authorities often establish bonded areas as a pretext for tax evasion or outright smuggling. The result is that the China Customs Administration makes controls in bonded areas so tight and inflexible that investors have little incentive to operate there. For instance, though Futian has independent access from Hong Kong, it is often easier to enter Futian from Shenzhen than to do so directly from Hong Kong.[1]

Bonded areas are run by special management boards, and this implies that foreign investors have to deal with an additional layer of bureaucracy. In the case of Futian, the board appears to be more interested in short-term gains of its own than in long-run economic development. In fact, long before there were any plans for the Futian bonded area, Hong Kong investors leased land in the Futian area because its proximity to Hong Kong implies good development potential. This alerted Shenzhen authorities to the value of Futian, and they dishonoured the leases and took back the land to develop Futian into a bonded area.[2] Futian's development was far below what was expected, partly because of excessive fees levied by the board. Another problem is that the board formed companies of its own to compete with private investors. For instance, after private investors found out that freight consolidation was profitable in Futian, the board formed its own consolidation company.

The problem is that Shenzhen has monopoly power because it is the only locality adjacent to Hong Kong, and some officials are understandably more interested in exploiting this monopoly power to their own advantage than in long-term economic development.

Cross-Border Industrial Park

Due to the shortage of land in Hong Kong, there have been proposals to establish an industrial park in Shenzhen just adjacent to Hong Kong. Besides providing cheap land, the park would also be able to tap the labour and engineering skills of China and the efficient supporting services of Hong Kong.

However, an industrial park in Shenzhen would have to be managed by the Shenzhen authorities and the China Customs Administration, which are not known for their efficiency. In fact, under efficient management, Futian could function as such an industrial park. Since Futian has not prospered, there is little hope that the proposed park would prosper either.

The alternative would be to establish the park in the border areas of Hong Kong. The park would then be under Hong Kong management. Textile and clothing manufacturers who are politically powerful in Hong Kong put forth such a proposal. Their goal was to import cheap labour from China to utilize Hong Kong's textile and clothing quotas. The Hong Kong government turned down the proposal, as it would have give importing countries an excuse to cut Hong Kong's quotas. In any case, since the textile and clothing industries are labour-intensive, they will naturally decline with rising wages, and there is little reason to rescue sunset industries.

Setting aside the textile and clothing industries, there is good reason to look into the establishment of an industrial park for more advanced industries in the border areas of Hong Kong. Besides cheap labour, China also has a vast army of engineers and considerable strength in research and development. Hong Kong has ample land in the border areas, as it has kept a vast band of land along the border undeveloped to strengthen border control. With the miraculous economic development in Shenzhen, there have been few desperate refugees risking their lives to scale fences to come into Hong Kong. Illegal immigrants have used safer channels, such as high-speed motor boats. It is time for the Hong Kong government to reconsider land use in the border areas.

Shenzhen as a Bonded Area

Shenzhen has plans to become a huge bonded area or free trade zone through "opening the first line and tightening the second line". However, the plan is fraught with technical difficulties and may have highly undesirable consequences.

It will be very difficult to prevent the smuggling of people and goods between Shenzhen and the rest of China. Even if this technical difficulty can be overcome, tightening the second line implies that people and goods going from Hong Kong to China via Shenzhen will have to go through customs twice. Moreover, the rest of China will lose, because its links with Shenzhen will be weakened.

There is now rampant smuggling between the Mainland and Hong Kong despite strenuous efforts to crack down on the illegal traffic on both sides of the border. Once Shenzhen becomes a free-trade zone, luxury consumer goods will be able to enter Shenzhen freely, and Hong Kong's smuggling rings will move their operations to Shenzhen. Policing will be extremely difficult, because the length of the second line is thrice the length of the Hong Kong–Shenzhen border, and the length of the coast of Shenzhen is roughly the same as that of the second line.[3] Moreover, the second line has been poorly designed; it goes through some built-up areas and has no roads for patrolling in many places. Smugglers can easily cut the fence and walk through.

Presently, smugglers have to deal with the police forces of two different systems — Hong Kong's and China's. Once the smuggling rings move to the bonded area of Shenzhen, they will only have to deal with or bribe the police of one system. In August 1992 Shenzhen sold application forms for new share subscriptions. Nearly a million people rushed into Shenzhen, resulting in demonstrations and riots. The episode shows that the second line is powerless to stem the tide of would-be immigrants.

After Shenzhen becomes a free-trade zone, goods going from Hong Kong to the area north of Shenzhen will have to go through customs twice: once when the goods go from Hong Kong into Shenzhen, and a second time when they go through the second line. The economic losses connected to going through customs twice are considerable. According to a 1992 survey of the Hong Kong General Chamber of Commerce, Hong Kong trucks going into Shenzhen have to wait an average of an hour, resulting in losses of HK$30 billion a year (*Hong Kong Economic Times*, 22 May 1992).

Presently, people leaving Shenzhen through the second line do not have to go through customs, but trucks leaving Shenzhen to go inland must do so. This is because Shenzhen can import selected amounts of consumer goods for use in Shenzhen at half the official tariff rates. As the quantity of goods entitled to partial tariff exemptions is strictly controlled, the problem of smuggling is not serious, and trucks do not have to line up to pass the second line.

Once Shenzhen becomes a free-trade zone, both people and trucks leaving it to go inland will have to be inspected, and congestion at the second line will be a big problem. Some commentators have opined that the containers of Hong Kong's trucks could be inspected and sealed at the Hong Kong–Shenzhen border, and that there would then be no need for another inspection at the second line. However, on a container truck, there are plenty of areas such as the driver's compartment that cannot be sealed. It will be difficult to avoid the need for a second inspection. The only way to do so will be to build a sealed highway through Shenzhen, but the feasibility and cost of such a project have yet to be studied.

The undesirable consequences of creating the huge bonded area of Shenzhen would not arise in Futian or in other bonded areas. Hong Kong trucks going north into China have to pass through Shenzhen, but they do not have to go through Futian or other bonded areas, and the problem of going through customs twice will not arise. Moreover, Futian or other bonded areas do not have permanent residents. Therefore, they do not have to impose strict controls on visitors to stem illegal immigration. Similarly, smuggling rings cannot easily use them as bases of operation.

Last, turning Shenzhen into a bonded zone may invite the animosity of inland areas. Beijing's official policy is to let selected areas "get rich first" and to then encourage laggards to catch up. However, if the favoured area encloses itself with a "second line" after getting rich and then imposes strict controls on poor cousins coming in, the policy will weaken the diffusion of the developmental process from the developed area to the less developed areas. The policy can easily lead to economic polarization.

Co-ordination of Infrastructure Developments

It has been pointed out that there are too many seaports and airports in the Pearl River Delta. Within just a couple of years after Deng's 1992 southern tour, Beijing had approved the construction of three deep-water ports adjacent to Hong Kong, namely Yantian in Shenzhen, Huizhou port in Daya Bay, and Gaolan port in

Zhuhai. These are in addition to the existing Guangzhou port and Shekou port in Shenzhen (Sung, Liu, Wong, and Lau, 1995, pp. 193–198). Though the Hong Kong port is congested, and there is the need for another port in the Pearl River Delta, there will be inadequate freight to supply so many deep-water, ocean-going ports.

A successful international port must have sufficient freight to attract shipping companies to make frequent calls. A large and busy port tends to be efficient because of economies of agglomeration. An increase in freight will imply a busier shipping schedule, which will in turn attract more freight to the port, as the freight can be shipped out speedily. The process snowballs until the port is congested. The need to develop a new port then comes into play.

Hong Kong has been the busiest container port in the world for some time. It handled 13.4 million containers in 1996. A minimum freight volume of 1.5 million containers a year is needed for the efficient operation of a container port (Sung, Liu, Wong and Lau, 1995, p. 196). All the Chinese ports near Hong Kong have quite a long way to go to reach the threshold of 1.5 million containers a year. Yantian, which has the most potential, handled 0.3 million containers in 1996. Shekou only handled 0.1 million containers in 1996. The Huizhou and Gaolan ports have yet to take off, though some berths have already been completed. By spreading its efforts too thinly over too many ports, China is making it difficult for any of its port to compete with Hong Kong.

Like port construction in China, there is also duplication in airport facilities within the country. Within a region of 200 square kilometres in the Pearl River Delta, there will be five international airports (Hong Kong, Macau, Shenzhen, and two airports in Guangzhou) and four local airports (Sung, Liu, Wong, and Lau, 1995, p. 198). Each local government looks after its own interest and wants a seaport or an airport as a showpiece. The result is excess capacity and duplication of facilities.

Co-ordination and Competition
Though improvements in planning and co-ordination can eliminate

some duplication of facilities, a certain amount of excess capacity and duplication is essential for competition. Planners may be able to rule out the more obvious failure cases, but they may not have enough information to pinpoint the successful ones. For instance, the choice of Shekou as an ocean-going port appears to be a planning mistake because of its shallow waterway, which needs dredging. However, planners are probably not able to decide between Yantian and Gaolan, as both of them have potential. A certain amount of trial and error is necessary, and no amount of feasibility studies can replace market tests. The problem with ports and airports in the Pearl River Delta is not excess capacity *per se*, but the ability of local governments to subsidize ports and airports from the public purse. Public subsidy implies that there is no real market test, as a loss-making port or airport can continue to operate.

It has been pointed out that the participation of foreign capital in infrastructure development will imply more efficient resource use, as foreign investors will help government officials evaluate the cost-effectiveness of infrastructure projects. Overdevelopment of local airports in the Pearl River Delta has been attributed to the lack of participation of foreign capital (Sung, Liu, Wong, and Lau, 1995, p. 202).

Recently, China has allowed increasing participation of foreign capital in infrastructure projects, including seaports. Hong Kong International Terminals Limited (HIT) has invested in the ports of Yantian, Shanghai, and Gaolan, as well as in other feeder ports in the Pearl River Delta (Cheng and Wong, 1997, p. 61). Swire Pacific and Peninsular & Oriental Stream Navigation Co. (P&O) has acquired 50% of the Shekou Container Terminal.

Yantian has been growing rapidly and has the most potential among all South China ports as far as developing into a major container port is concerned. The design capacity of Yantian will reach 1.7 million containers in 1999. However, Yantian needs time to grow, and Hong Kong will remain the major hub for years to come, with Yantian serving as a subsidiary port (Cheng and Wong, 1997, pp. 62–68). Hong Kong handled 93% of Guangdong's cargo in 1996. Though the share will likely diminish, the absolute volume of cargo handled by Hong Kong will continue to rise.

Co-ordination of Infrastructure Development after 1997

The Sino-British dispute on the Patten proposals for constitutional reform in Hong Kong may have hindered co-ordination of infrastructure development between Hong Kong and China. For instance, the construction of both Hong Kong's new airport and of container terminal number 9 were held up for a while due to the Sino-British dispute. The reversion of Hong Kong to China should lead to better co-ordination of infrastructure developments in the Pearl River Delta.

However, it should not be assumed that Hong Kong's reversion will solve the problem of co-ordination. For instance, neither Beijing nor the provincial government of Guangdong has been able to rationalize the many airports and seaports put forward by the local governments of the Pearl River Delta. In Shenzhen alone there are two ocean-going ports, Yantian and Shekou, which is one too many. As is mentioned in Chapter 3, the Shekou industrial export zone was formed one year earlier than the Shenzhen SEZ and was managed by the China Merchants Company, which is based in Hong Kong. Though Shekou was incorporated into Shenzhen, Shekou continued to be administered by the China Merchants Company for a while. Shenzhen has been unable to stop the construction of the Shekou port.

Bureaucratic co-ordination may not be powerful enough to override local interests. Even if it is, it is unlikely to be highly rational and efficient. Market co-ordination will generate better results as long as local governments refrain from giving undue subsidies to infrastructure. The participation of private capital and foreign investors in infrastructure should be encouraged as much as possible.

Notes

1. Information obtained from interview with investors in Futian.

2. The down payments for the land were returned to the investors without interest after long delays.

3. *Hong Kong Economic Daily*, 24 and 25, April 1992.

CHAPTER 8

Problems and Prospects of the China Circle

While the growth of the China Circle has been extremely rapid, and there have been many rosy projections of the future, the China Circle also faces a host of problems, both economic and political. Four such problems are discussed in this final chapter. They are:

1. The difficulty of implementing further reforms of the Chinese economic systems;
2. Problems adjusting to China's export drive in the world market, especially in terms of trade friction with the United States and other Western countries;
3. Tensions across the Taiwan Strait; and,
4. Maintaining prosperity in Hong Kong after 1997.

Difficulty Implementing Further Reforms

After eighteen years of economic reforms and opening, the Chinese reforms have reached a cross-roads. Most of the easy-to-implement reforms (agricultural reforms, privatization of small firms) have been completed, and the those remaining (reform of large, state-owned enterprises, banking reforms, reforms of the fiscal and monetary system) are going to be much more difficult to put into practice. The lack of thorough reform will limit foreign investment in China, especially in industries selling to the domestic market and also in service sectors such as banking, finance, and telecommunications.

Hong Kong and Taiwan's investments in China have largely been confined to using China as an export base. This can be attributed to the shallowness of China's reforms. China merely provides cheap land and labour, and all the other ingredients such as raw materials, management, industrial design, marketing, and financing are provided externally. Moreover, the foreign investor can recoup the investment as the product is exported, earning foreign exchange in return. Foreign investors who invest in industries selling to the domestic market find it more difficult to recoup their investment due to China's foreign exchange controls. Investors in sectors such as banking, finance, and telecommunications will face difficulties, as such sectors tend to be highly regulated. The speed at which these sectors open to foreign investors will be limited by the pace of China's reforms.

Problems of Adjustment in the World Market

Although the China Circle is not an inward-looking trade bloc, the scale of China's entry into the world market has raised problems of adjustment in the world economy. China's exports are overly concentrated in selling labour-intensive products to the American market. The size of the U.S.–China bilateral deficit is second only to the U.S.–Japan deficit. Though the size of bilateral trade deficits has little economic meaning and significance, it can easily lead to severe political problems and trade friction.

Protectionism is a problem for China. China's most favoured nations (MFN) status in the United States is subject to renewal debates every year. China is running up against its quota of textiles and clothing exports, and the number of anti-dumping charges against China is increasing fast. Almost every year, China is high on the hit list of U.S. Section 301 or Super 301 investigations.

However, the problem on the demand side has been exaggerated. Due to the relocation of export-oriented industries of Hong Kong and Taiwan to China, the American trade deficit with China has increased tremendously. At the same time, American bilateral deficits with Hong Kong and Taiwan have declined. Though the total exports of the China Circle to the United States have gone up (as the relocated firms often expand in scale with the availability of cheap labour and land in China), the total exports of the United States to the China Circle have also increased markedly because of Taiwan's trade liberalization and China's rapid growth. The net result is that, despite the absolute size of the United States' overall trade deficit with the China Circle having grown from US$22.6 billion in 1989 to US$57.2 billion in 1997, the size of the deficit relative to U.S. exports has only risen from 7% to 8.4%.

Trade frictions can be avoided if China liberalizes its imports of commodities and services. As services can usually only be provided on site, the liberalization of service trade often implies the liberalization of foreign investment in service industries. Such liberalization would give rise to many investment opportunities and would also imply a much higher degree of integration of the China Circle.

Even if China wants to liberalize its imports of goods and services, the industrial bases in Hong Kong and Taiwan are too narrow to meet China's demands. Hong Kong and Taiwan are not likely to become China's foremost suppliers. Granted that China may become the largest market for Hong Kong and Taiwan, the reverse is unlikely to be the case. When China liberalizes its trade policy, its imports of final goods will increase relative to its import of semi-manufactured goods, and it will probably shift its imports away from Hong Kong and Taiwan to Japan and the West. China has to look out of the China Circle for its capital goods, technology, and market. The liberalization of China's imports will thus imply rich opportunities for East Asia and the world.

Tensions across the Taiwan Straits

Since China's military exercises in the Taiwan Straits in late 1995 and early 1996, public sentiment in Taiwan has been tilting towards independence. Taipei will not accept the formula of "one country, two systems" if it has any options, because it does not want to be relegated to the status of a provincial government.

Pro-independence forces may gain ascendency in Taiwan. If China perceives that the situation is getting out of hand, it may use force or impose an embargo against Taiwan, and Hong Kong will have to join the embargo. Hostility across the Taiwan Straits would be a disaster for Hong Kong.

Hong Kong's Stability after 1997

Though the economic freedoms of Hong Kong are spelt out in great detail in the Sino-British Declaration on the future of Hong Kong, it must be remembered that "one country, two systems" is an untried formula and that the future stability and prosperity of Hong Kong is not assured. As Hong Kong is the pivot of the economic integration of the China Circle, the consequences of Hong Kong's demise for China and the China Circle can be very serious.

The workability of "one country, two systems" lies more in the political and social realms than in the economic realm. The political problem is that China has to resist tremendous temptation and pressure to intervene in the internal affairs of Hong Kong. As long as it can respect Hong Kong's autonomy, the economic fundamentals are likely to work in Hong Kong's favour. As the author has discussed elsewhere, the prospect of Hong Kong as China's middleman is bright (Sung 1991, pp. 28–42). China will further decentralize its trading system and create greater opportunities of intermediation for the Hong Kong middleman. Moreover, there are significant economies of scale and economies of agglomeration in trading activity, and it is very difficult for other cities such as Singapore or Shanghai to compete with Hong Kong, because Hong Kong is the established centre for China's trade. The existence of economies of scale in intermediation would enhance the demand for the middleman, as small firms will not be able to trade efficiently.

Hong Kong's Competitors

The competitors for Hong Kong's regional role include Singapore, Taipei, and Shanghai. Of the three cities, Singapore is the toughest competitor, as the quality of its skills, facilities, and infrastructure rivals that of Hong Kong's. However, Singapore and Hong Kong are more complementary than competitive because they serve different regions. Hong Kong and Singapore are separated by a four-hour flight. Singapore is ideally situated to serve Southeast Asia, whereas Hong Kong is better located to serve China, Taiwan, Korea, or even Japan. Though both Southeast and Northeast Asia are very dynamic, the Northeast Asian economy is much larger than that of Southeast Asia, and this gives Hong Kong an edge over Singapore as a regional service centre. Moreover, Hong Kong has a greater range of skills, as the size of the Hong Kong economy is 2.5 times that of Singapore.

Singapore cannot seriously challenge the lead of Hong Kong as the gateway to China because of location. In fact, Singapore has become increasingly dependent on Hong Kong for its trade with China (Sung 1991, pp. 135–136).

Taipei as a Competitor of Hong Kong

Taipei aspires to become a regional financial, corporate, and transportation centre and can pose a serious threat to Hong Kong because of proximity. Taipei is located in the same region as Hong Kong and it is only a one-hour flight away.

Taiwan has huge investments in and a big trading network throughout Southeast Asia. Although its investment in China is only a fraction of that of Hong Kong, Taiwan's investment in the Mainland has grown very fast and may rival that of Hong Kong in the long run. Moreover, Taiwanese speak better Mandarin than Hong Kong Chinese do, and Taiwanese businesspeople are more adept at dealing with bureaucrats because Taiwan's business environment is similar to China's.

Presently, Taipei does not realize its potential, because of the official policy of no direct links with the Mainland. Taiwan's trade and investment with the Mainland are largely handled through Hong Kong, and Taiwan's policy strengthens Hong Kong's lead as a regional service centre. Taipei can only be a serious competitor to

Hong Kong in the very long run when direct Taiwan–China links are fully developed. Even when these links are fully developed, Taipei will still face challenges from Hong Kong. Taipei's service skills lag far behind those of Hong Kong, and Taiwan's heavily regulated environment is not conducive to the development of Taipei as a regional service centre. Moreover, Hong Kong's natural hinterland, Guangdong, is much more dynamic than Taiwan's natural hinterland, Fujian.

Last, it must be remembered that Hong Kong and Taiwan are in some ways complementary. Taiwan is stronger in engineering and industrial skills, while Hong Kong is stronger in finance, shipping, and legal services.

Shanghai as a Competitor of Hong Kong

Shanghai has the advantage of location, as it is situated at the mouth of the Yangzi basin which is the largest and most prosperous river basin in China. Although Shanghai is set to become the domestic financial centre of China, it cannot compete with Hong Kong as a regional or international centre unless the Renminbi achieves convertibility on the capital account. Although China has achieved convertibility in merchandise trade, capital account convertibility will take much longer. The experiences of trade and exchange rate liberalization in developing countries has repeatedly demonstrated that capital account convertibility takes a long time to achieve.

The development of infrastructure and services skills is a time-consuming and capital-intensive process. Moreover, the development of services is highly dependent on the regulatory environment. Given China's corrupt, inefficient, and immense bureaucracy, developing an efficient international service centre will be very difficult.

Last, Shanghai does not have a good port because of the silting of the Yangzi River. Ships over 50,000 tons can only enter Shanghai (or any port along the Yangzi) at high tide.

Though Shanghai is emerging as the business centre of the Yangzi Delta, it cannot challenge Hong Kong's position as a regional and international business and financial centre.

Table 8.1 shows the share of China's trade via Hong Kong and via Shanghai since 1979. The share of China's *exports* via Shanghai declined from 26.9% to a low of 14% in 1990 and then rebounded to 18% by 1997. On the other hand, the share of China's exports via Hong Kong to third countries rose from 7.3% in 1979 to a peak of 49.7% in 1993 and then declined to 38% by 1997. The share of China's exports via Hong Kong in 1997 was more than twice that of Shanghai.

The share of China's *imports* via Hong Kong rose continually from an insignificant 1.7% in 1979 to a record 40.3% in 1997. This is in sharp contrast to the rapid decline of Shanghai's share.

The share of China's *trade* (imports plus exports) via Hong Kong rose rapidly from 4.3% in 1979 to a peak of 41.5% in 1996 and then declined marginally to 39% in 1997. This is in sharp contrast to the rapid decline of Shanghai's share.

Table 8.1 greatly understates Hong Kong's middleman role in China's trade, because transshipments and direct shipments handled by Hong Kong firms are not included in trade figures. In recent years, Hong Kong traders have substituted direct shipments for re-exports. The slight fall in the share of China's trade via Hong Kong (in the form of re-exports) in 1997 is not an indication of the decline of Hong Kong's middleman role in China's trade.

It is amazing that, eighteen years after China's opening, Hong Kong's shares are still so high. In 1997 Hong Kong still handled two-fifths of China's trade in the form of re-exports, and Hong Kong's share would be two-thirds if transshipments, direct shipments, and trade with Hong Kong itself were included. Hong Kong also accounted for 45% of the 1997 utilized FDI in China.

The continuing high shares of Hong Kong in China's trade and investment show the importance of economies of scale and agglomeration in trading and service activities. In fact, economies of scale

Chapter 8

Table 8.1
China's Trade via Shanghai and Hong Kong, 1979–97
(US$ million)

	Via Shanghai[a]			China's Trade via Hong Kong with Third Countries[b]			China's Trade with Hong Kong[c]		
	Total Trade	Exports	Imports	Total Trade	Exports	Imports	Total Trade	Exports	Imports
1979	–	3,675	–	1,265	1002	263	3,428	3,045	383
	–	(26.9)	–	(4.3)	(7.3)	(1.7)	(11.7)	(22.3)	(2.5)
1985	14,873	4,908	9,965	9,841	3,934	5,907	15,306	7,449	7,857
	(21.4)	(18.0)	(23.6)	(14.2)	(14.4)	(14.0)	(22.0)	(27.3)	(18.6)
1987	15,635	6,601	9,034	17,231	9,562	7,669	26,065	14,775	11,290
	(18.9)	(16.7)	(20.9)	(20.9)	(24.3)	(17.8)	(31.6)	(37.5)	(26.1)
1989	19,437	7,711	11,726	34,623	21,355	13,268	43,248	24,432	18,816
	(17.4)	(14.7)	(19.8)	(31.0)	(40.7)	(22.4)	(38.8)	(46.6)	(31.8)
1990	17,289	8,662	8,627	39,728	25,509	14,219	49,833	29,528	20,305
	(15.0)	(14.0)	(16.2)	(34.4)	(41.1)	(26.7)	(43.2)	(47.6)	(38.1)
1991	20,409	10,151	10,258	51,940	32,284	19,656	63,342	36,711	26,631
	(15.1)	(14.1)	(16.1)	(38.3)	(44.9)	(30.8)	(46.7)	(51.1)	(41.7)
1992	25,145	11,964	13,181	67,413	40,220	27,193	79,323	44,187	35,136
	(15.2)	(14.1)	(16.4)	(30.7)	(47.3)	(34.9)	(47.9)	(52.0)	(45.1)
1993	30,931	13,977	16,954	81,046	45,555	35,491	93,848	50,165	43,683
	(15.8)	(15.2)	(16.3)	(41.4)	(49.7)	(34.1)	(47.9)	(54.7)	(42.0)
1994	36,246	18,938	17,308	94,823	53,047	41,776	108,372	58,702	49,670
	(15.3)	(15.7)	(15.0)	(40.1)	(43.9)	(36.1)	(45.8)	(48.6)	(42.9)
1995	48,138	25,608	22,530	111,490	61,808	49,682	125,204	67,300	57,904
	(17.1)	(17.2)	(17.1)	(39.7)	(41.6)	(37.6)	(44.6)	(45.3)	(43.8)
1996	52,869	27,213	25,656	120,365	66,350	54,015	133,130	71,148	61,982
	(18.2)	(18.0)	(18.5)	(41.5)	(43.9)	(38.9)	(45.9)	(47.1)	(44.6)
1997	58,682	33,450	25,232	126,858	69,524	51,334	140,777	75,194	65,583
	(18.1)	(18.3)	(17.7)	(39.0)	(38.0)	(40.3)	(43.3)	(41.1)	(46.1)

Sources: Trade via Shanghai: Data since 1993 come from *China Customs Statistics*; Data before 1993 come from *The Foreign Economic Statistical Yearbook of Shanghai*; Shanghai Statistical Bureau.
China's Trade via Hong Kong and with Hong Kong: *Hong Kong External Trade*, Census and Statistics Department, Hong Kong, various issues.

Notes: Figures in bracket represent percentage share of China's total. China's exports to (imports from) Hong Kong are taken to be Hong Kong's imports from (exports to) China. Price differences between f.o.b. and c.i.f. are ignored because they are small.
(a) Includes products imported / exported by other provinces via Shanghai's Customs.
(b) Includes only China's trade with third countries in the form of Hong Kong re-exports.
(c) Includes also China's exports retained in Hong Kong and China imports of Hong Kong goods in addition to China's trade via Hong Kong.

and agglomeration characterize most economic activities, including agriculture, manufacturing, transportation, trading, business services, and financial services. Agglomeration leads to rising land prices, which eventually stop the tendency of agglomeration. Agriculture is the first activity to move out of the city, because it is the most land-intensive. Manufacturing is the second activity to move, and Hong Kong manufacturing has largely moved to South China. Transportation is the next activity to be affected, as ports and airports are also land-intensive. The high costs of Hong Kong's new airport and container ports are expected in land-scarce Hong Kong. The new Hong Kong airport will be twenty times as expensive as the Huangtian airport in Shenzhen, which will also have two runways when it is fully developed. Were it not for political barriers, it would make more sense to put Hong Kong's new airport in Shenzhen. However, China's customs administration is not noted for its efficiency, and it would be risky for Hong Kong to locate its new airport in Shenzhen unless China thoroughly reformed and modernized its customs administration. It is not realistic to expect such reforms to be completed in the near future. However, when they are completed, it will make sense for Hong Kong to divert some of its cargo traffic to China.

In handling China's trade, Hong Kong firms have recently substituted direct shipment for re-exports via Hong Kong. This is natural, as transportation via Hong Kong can be expensive because of congested container ports and airports. Congestion also generates huge external costs for the residents of Hong Kong. Allowing nearly half of China's rapidly increasing trade to be transported via Hong Kong's tiny territory forever is not in Hong Kong's best interest. Moreover, the average gross margins earned by Hong Kong's trading firms (16.1% for exporting Chinese goods and 12.6% for exporting third country goods) appear to be similar for re-exports through Hong Kong and for offshore trade (Hong Kong Trade Development Council, 1996, pp. 8–9).

Trading, business services, and financial services will be least affected by rising land prices and wages, because such activities are neither land- nor labour-intensive. New York and London long ago lost their comparative advantage in manufacturing, but their positions in trading, business, and finance remain formidable.

Hong Kong's shares in China's trade and investment are so high that they are unlikely to rise further. The shares are likely to decline, as China is building many ports, and many foreign multinationals are investing in China. In the long run, China is likely to overcome its transportation bottlenecks and acquire modern trading skills. While China may even clean up its bureaucracy, it will still rely on Hong Kong for trade, financial, and business services, because of economies of scale and agglomeration.

China has established many trading companies in Hong Kong, showing that the territory's efficiency in trading is well recognized. Some Hong Kong traders fear competition from mainland trading companies in Hong Kong. However, because of economies of scale and agglomeration, the situation is not a zero-sum game — the arrival of mainland trading companies further enhances the position of Hong Kong as a trading centre.

Prospects of the China Circle

Economic forces point to a rapid continuation of economic integration of the China Circle. Though there are political uncertainties such as the stability of China in the post-Deng era, doubts about the viability of Hong Kong after 1997, and possible hostilities over the Taiwan Strait, the economic fundamentals of the China Circle are strong.

Because of the many differences in the political, legal, and economic systems of the Mainland on the one hand and those of "capitalist China" (Hong Kong and Taiwan) on the other, the economic integration of the Mainland with capitalist China will be highly uneven. Integration will proceed rapidly in some areas but slowly in others. Between the Mainland and capitalist China, controls on movements of goods are relatively liberal, whereas controls on capital and foreign exchange are stricter, and controls on migration are the strictest. Integration of the commodity market between the Mainland and capitalist China will proceed rapidly because of the relatively mild controls over the flow of goods. However, even for the commodity market, one should distinguish between export-processing industries and import-competing industries. The outward-processing operations of capitalist China on the Mainland have developed extremely rapidly because their products are exported, and they are not hampered by China's foreign exchange controls. The growth of external investment in China's import-competing industries will necessarily be slower as a result of China's foreign exchange controls.

Similarly, the integration of the Mainland's and capitalist China's service industries will be slow, because most services cannot be exported and are sold in the domestic market. Moreover, services are performed on people and require people-to-people contact. The controls of capitalist China on migration from the Mainland will hamper the full integration of services.

The integration of the financial markets of the Mainland and capitalist China will also be quite slow, as China's foreign exchange controls on the capital account will likely be quite strict even in the medium term. The integration of the labour markets of the Mainland and capitalist China will probably be very slow because of controls on migration.

The China Circle and the World Trading System

The economic reality of the trio is that the United States is its largest market and Japan is its largest supplier of capital goods and technology. An inward-looking bloc of the trio excluding the United States and Japan would thus not be in the trio's long-term interest.

Though Hong Kong is irrevocably integrated with the Mainland, it must be remembered that Hong Kong can function as the bridge linking the Mainland and the world only because Hong Kong is also irrevocably integrated with the world economy. An inward-looking bloc involving Hong Kong and the Mainland would be detrimental to both.

China has actively participated in the trade liberalization process of the APEC (Asian-Pacific Economic Community). China's commitments to the APEC enhance the credibility of China's reform and trade liberalization policies. The APEC opens the markets of its members to Chinese exports and also provides a forum for interaction among members of the trio.

However, the APEC is at best an imperfect substitute for the WTO. The APEC cannot give China recourse to the protectionist actions of non-APEC members. Moreover, the APEC process is fuzzy and less rule-based than that of the WTO. For enhancement of credibility of trade liberalization, APEC membership counts much less than WTO membership because APEC allows its members to make vague commitments.

The advantage of the APEC process is its flexibility. As China's trade regime is far from "GATTable", it would be rash for it to jump immediately into the rule-based WTO system. To use Deng Xiaoping's imagery, the APEC process provides the stepping stones over which China can cross the treacherous river of economic reforms into the land of the WTO.

To achieve the integration of the trio, the pivotal role of Hong Kong as an efficient middleman and the importance of the unilateral trade liberalization of the Mainland and Taiwan have clearly been important. The integration of the trio will continue to be largely market driven, though consultation through the APEC, through semi-official organizations such as the Straits Foundation in Taiwan, or through privately sponsored forums to improve the information flow and to discuss possible policy co-ordination, will all be useful. WTO membership for both the Mainland and Taiwan would give the integration of the trio a tremendous boost. Institutional discriminatory preferences are utopian and counter-productive, and unilateral discriminatory preferences are "unGATTable" and detrimental.

In the long run, the best economic and political policy for Beijing is national treatment for all. However, given the many distortions of the Chinese economy, this goal can be realized only gradually and in many stages. Needless to say, national treatment for all is the best policy for promotion of economic integration, not just for the trio, but also for the North Pacific region and for the world as a whole.

The China Circle and the East Asian Financial Crisis

The severity of the East Asian financial crisis starting mid-1997 have caught many investors and policy makers unprepared. China's stunning successes in exports and attracting FDI has eroded foreign exchange earnings in the ASEAN and contributed to the onset of the crisis. On 2 July 1997, the Thai baht was forced to devalue. The crisis rapidly spread to Malaysia, The Philippines, Indonesia, and South Korea. Financially sound economies such as Singapore, Hong Kong, and Taiwan have huge foreign exchange reserves and they were relatively unscathed in the initial stage of the crisis.

However, Taiwan, which has a huge current account surplus, let its currency depreciate in October 1997, and Taiwanese officials also publicly stated that the Hong Kong dollar and the Renminbi might be devalued. The events in Taiwan triggered attacks on the Hong Kong and Singaporean currencies, and stock markets worldwide also suffered severe losses. Taiwan's beggar-thy-neighbour policies have been widely criticized (Bergsten, 1997).

Unlike Taiwan, the Mainland and Hong Kong have stood firm and they have thus far maintained their exchange rates against the US dollar. Both governments have reiterated their determination to keep their exchange rates stable. Co-ordination in exchange rate policies between the Mainland and Hong Kong have contributed to financial stability in East Asia. The reversion of Hong Kong to China since July 1997 has facilitated policy co-ordination between Hong Kong and the Mainland.

The financial turmoils generated by the rapid depreciation of the Japanese Yen in mid-June, 1998 highlighted the importance of Mainland–Hong Kong policy co-ordination. Mainland officials repeatedly called upon the U.S., Japan and G-7 nations to stabilize the Yen from 9 June to 17 June, 1998. Tung Chee-hwa, chief executive of Hong Kong, was then visiting Australia and New Zealand and he echoed such calls. On 15 June 1998, the Hong Kong Monetary Authority stated that it would use its reserves to buy Yen if G-7 nations would do the same. On 17 June 1998, the Vice Minister of China's MOFTEC (Ministry of Foreign Trade and Economic Cooperation) hinted that China might renege on its pledge not to devalue if the Yen should continue to depreciate. The hint was widely perceived to be a threat on the U.S. and Japan to take action. On the same day, the U.S. and Japan intervened decisively in the New York market, and the exchange rate of the Yen to the US dollar rose from around 144 to 138. It was widely believed the pressure from China played an important part in U.S. intervention. The weaknesses of the Japanese economy has enhanced the role of China in the international economic arena. President Clinton has acknowledged the importance of the economic roles of the Mainland and Hong Kong in the East Asian financial crisis in his visit to China and Hong Kong in late June and early July of 1998.

Though the Mainland and Hong Kong have actively coordinated exchange-rate policies, it must be stressed that the Renminbi and the Hong Kong dollar are fundamentally different currencies. The Renminbi is not vulnerable to speculative attack because of capital controls. On the other hand, Hong Kong has complete freedom of capital movements and Hong Kong has been able to withstand attacks because of its financial strength. Since the establishment of the Linked Rate system in Hong Kong in October 1983, the exchange rate of the Hong Kong dollar to the US dollar has stood at 7.8 while the exchange rate of the Renminbi to the US dollar has depreciated from 1.5 in 1983 to 8.2 in 1998.

Hong Kong benefits from a fixed exchange rate much more than the Mainland because Hong Kong is a small economy where international transactions are relatively much more important. A fixed exchange rate system facilitates international transactions. While many small economies have pegged their currencies to those of their major economic partners, most large economies allow their exchange rates to float. For large economies, the burden of a fixed exchange rate system usually outweighs the gains. In the long run, the Mainland's interest is best served by a flexible rather than fixed exchange rate. However, in this financial crisis, exchange rate stability serves the interests of China as well as that of its neighbours. East Asian financial markets are very unstable in 1998, and devaluation of the Renminbi would trigger another round of devaluation and financial turmoils in East Asia. China has relatively little to gain from devaluation as long as the financial markets in East Asia are unstable.

Chinese exports are expected to stagnate in 1998 as a result of the East Asian financial crisis. In May 1998, Chinese exports dropped by 1.5%, the first negative growth registered in 22 months. It must be emphasized that, thus far, Asian's exports, which are potentially very competitive due to large depreciations, have not yet increased due to the dislocations of their financial systems. ASEAN exporters have difficulties in obtaining bank loans to finance exports. China's stagnated exports have been caused by declines in exports to East Asian markets rather than increased competition from ASEAN exports.

Once ASEAN financial markets stabilize, China's exports would face tremendous competition and the pressure on Renminbi to devalue would mount. By then, devaluation would be the preferred choice for China because there would be little risk of triggering fresh devaluation once stability returns to East Asia. China can fine tune the size of its devaluation because of its stringent capital controls. Speculators would not be able to attack the Renminbi.

Hong Kong would also benefit from such a devaluation. Once stability returns to East Asia, the psychological effect of a devaluation of the Renminbi on the Hong Kong dollar would be minimal. Hong Kong and the Mainland are complementary rather than competitive. As Hong Kong serves Mainland's trade and investment, a devaluation of the Renminbi should increase Mainland's trade, thereby benefiting Hong Kong.

The East Asian financial crisis has taken a heavy toll. Hong Kong's economic growth in 1998 is expected to be negative, and the Mainland's growth is expected to slow down by one or two percentage points. However, the Mainland and Hong Kong can alleviate a substantial part of the burden through judicious policy co-ordination.

Though the East Asian financial crisis has provided an opportunity for exchange-rate policy co-ordination between Hong Kong and the Mainland, the main impact of the crisis is to hamper the economic integration of the CEA as the crisis will slow down the process of economic reform and opening in the Mainland.

The Mainland is passing through the most difficult stage of its economic reform which involves the reform of banks, the financial system, and state-owned enterprises. Mainland's exports and inward FDI have stagnated due to the financial crisis, and this will lead to a fall in economic growth and a rise in unemployment. China's rate of unemployment is already high due to the closure of inefficient state-owned enterprises, and the additional unemployment generated by the crisis will be difficult to bear. China has already slowed down its reform of state-owned enterprises in August 1998 due to rising unemployment.

The East Asian financial crisis has demonstrated that the vast amounts of speculative capital in the world capital market can force financially sound economies, such as Taiwan and Singapore, to devalue. China's banking system has the same problems with bad debts as in Indonesia and Malaysia. The only reason that the Renminbi has escaped speculative attacks is that it is not convertible. After the East Asian crisis, China will slow down convertibility on its capital account. This will also hamper China's accession to the WTO.

Though the crisis will slow down opening and reform in China, the crisis has also highlighted the importance of thorough banking reforms. East Asian economies have been able to achieve rapid economic growth through hard work, high savings, and export-oriented industrialization. However, most East Asian economies have banking systems that are riddled by bad debts brought about by policy loans and nepotism. Fragile banking systems have turned out to be the Achilles heels of East Asian economies, and many of them have succumbed to speculative attacks. Even an economy as advanced as Japan has a banking system that is non-transparent and riddled with bad debts and nepotism. Japan has not been able to clean up its banking system even eight years after its market crashed in 1990. Under the influence of the East Asian value of consensual decision making, Japan has not been able to force insolvent banks to go bankrupt because that would be too harsh for the directors concerned. Likewise, Japan has not been able to clean up nepotism and corruption in its banking system. The case of Japan shows that reform of the banking system is difficult not only because of its economics, but also because banking reforms require political and cultural changes that go to the heart of East Asian political culture.

Among the Asian economies, Hong Kong and Singapore have transparent and sound banking and financial systems thanks to their colonial legacy. Viable and sound banking systems are rare in Asia. The East Asian financial crisis again underlines the strength of Hong Kong both as an international financial centre and as Mainland's gateway. The synergy effects between Hong Kong and South China, and indeed the role of Hong Kong as China's gateway, cannot easily be replaced by other cities.

China will soon enter the third decade of its reform era. China is trying to carry through the most difficult economic reforms which require *concomitant changes* that go against the grain of its political culture. If China can bite the bullet and complete its reforms, especially the reform of its banking system, then the Chinese Economic Area will rival the United States in economic strength in two or three decades. Otherwise, the further growth and integration of the Chinese Economic Area will be fraught with difficulties.

Bibliography

1. Bergsten, C. Fred (1997). "The Asian Monetary Crisis: Proposed Remedies," statement before the Committee on Banking and Financial Services, U.S. House of Representatives, November 13, 1997.

2. Census and Statistics Department (1993). "Hong Kong Residents Married in China," *Special Topics Report No. 8*: 115–126.

3. _____ (1996a). "Analysis of Hong Kong's Retained Imports, 1989–94," *Hong Kong Monthly Digest of Statistics*, Appendix F (February).

4. _____ (1996b). *External Investments in Hong Kong's Non-manufacturing Sectors, 1993 & 1994*, Hong Kong.

5. _____ (1997a). "Hong Kong Residents Married in China," *Special Topics Report No. 15*: 1–16.

6. _____ (1997b). "Hong Kong's Imports Measured on Free on Board (f.o.b.) Basis for 1996," *Hong Kong Monthly Digest of Statistics*, Appendix FB (December).

7. Cheng, Leonard K., and Wong Yue-Chim, Richard (1997). *Port Facilities and Container Handling Services (The Hong Kong Economic Policy Studies Series)*. Hong Kong: City University of Hong Kong Press.

8. Chia, Siow Yue (1993). "Motivating Forces in Subregional Economic Zones," Pacific Forum / CSIS Occasional Papers (December), Honolulu.

9. China Resources Group (1994). "China Resources Group: Striding into the New Century with Confidence," *The Hong Kong Chinese Enterprise*, Hong Kong Chinese Enterprise Association, pp. 47–49.

10. Hicks, John (1969). *A Theory of Economic History*. London: Oxford University Press.

11. Ho, S. P. S. and Huenemann, R. W. (1984). *China's Open Door Policy: The Quest for Foreign Technology and Capital*. Vancouver: University of British Columbia Press.

12. Hong Kong Trade Development Council (1992). "Hong Kong's Economic Relationship with Taiwan", Hong Kong (February).

13. _____ (1996). "Hong Kong's Trade and Trade Supporting Services", Hong Kong (April).

14. Hong Kong Trade Development Council (1998). "The Rise in Offshore Trade and Offshore Investment," Hong Kong (March).

15. Jao, Y. C. (1983). "Hong Kong's Role in Financing China's Modernization," in *China and Hong Kong, the Economic Nexus*, A. J. Youngson, ed. Hong Kong: Oxford University Press, pp. 12–76.

16. Kao, Chang and Sung, Yun-Wing (1995). *An Empirical Study of Indirect Trade between Taiwan and Mainland China*, Mainland Committee of Taiwan Government, Taipei (September).

17. Lin, Tzong-biau and Kan, Chak-yuen (1996). "Chinese Firms and the Hong Kong Economy," *Asian Studies*, No. 17 (April): 130–176 (Center for Asian Studies, Chu Hai College, Hong Kong) (in Chinese).

18. Lucas, Robert (1985). *The Mechanics of Economic Development*. Marshall Lecture, Cambridge University, Cambridge.

19. Qiu, Hong (1996). "Openness and Economic Growth in China," M. Phil. thesis, Chinese University of Hong Kong (mimeo).

20. Liu, Qingwen (1994). "Hong Kong PRC-invested Enterprises before and after 1997," *The Hong Kong Chinese Enterprise*, Hong Kong Chinese Enterprise Association, pp. 39–44.

21. Naughton, Barry (1997). "Economic Policy Reform in PRC and Taiwan," in *The China Circle: Economics and Electronics in the PRC, Taiwan, and Hong Kong*, Naughton, Barry, ed., Washington, D. C.: Brookings Institute, pp. 81–110.

22. Ni, Nick (1994). *Asian Perspectives: China's Expanding Economic Interests in Hong Kong*, Nomura Research Institute Hong Kong Limited, Vol. 11, No. 6 (December).

23. Scalapino, Robert A. (1992). "The United States and Asia: Future Prospects," *Foreign Affairs*, Winter 1991/92: 19–40.

24. Shen, George (1993). "China's Investment in Hong Kong," in *The Other Hong Kong Report 1993*, Choi Po-king and Ho Lok-sang, eds. Hong Kong: The Chinese University Press, pp. 425–454.

25. Sung, Yun-Wing (1991). *The China–Hong Kong Connection: The Key to China's Open-Door Policy*. Cambridge: Cambridge University Press.

26. _____ (1992). "Non-institutional Economic Integration via Cultural Affinity: The Case of Mainland China, Taiwan, and Hong Kong," *Occasional Paper No. 13* (July), Hong Kong Institute of Asia-Pacific Studies, The Chinese University of Hong Kong.

27. Sung, Yun-Wing (1996). "Chinese Outward Investment in Hong Kong: Trends, Prospects, and Policy Implications," *OECD Development Centre, Technical Papers*, No. 113 (July).

28. _____, Liu, Pak-Wai, Wong, Yue-Chim Richard, and Lau, Pui-King. (1995). *The Fifth Dragon: The Emergence of the Pearl River Delta*. Singapore: Addison-Wesley.

29. United Nations (1996). *World Investment Report 1996. New York.*

30. Wakabayashi, Masahiro (1990). "Relations between Taiwan and China During the 1980s, Viewed from the Taiwan Perspective," Jetro's *China Newsletter* No. 87, (July–August): 6–16.

31. Wang, Xianzhang (1994). "Expand Insurance Business at an Accelerated Speed," *Hong Kong Chinese Enterprise*, Hong Kong Chinese Enterprise Association, Hong Kong, pp. 50–55.

32. Wei, Shang-Jin (1995). "The Open Door Policy and China's Rapid Growth: Evidence from City-Level Data", in *Growth Theories in Light of the East Asian Experience*, Ito, Takatoshi and Krueger, Anne, eds. Chicago: University of Chicago Press, pp. 73–104.

33. _____ (1996). "How Taxing is Corruption on International Investors" (mimeograph).

34. Xu, Jiatun (1993). "Xu Jiatun Hong Kong Memoir," *Hong Kong United Daily*, Hong Kong (in Chinese).

35. Yamamura, Kozo (1976), "General Trading Companies in Japan: Their Origins and Growth," in *Japanese Industrialization and Its Social Consequences*, Hugh Patrick, ed. Berkeley: University of California Press.

36. Yeh, Milton (1995). "Ask a Tiger for its Hide? Taiwan's Approach to Economic Transaction across the Straits," in *Southern China, Hong Kong, and Taiwan*, Khanna, Jane, ed. Washington D. C.: The Center for Strategic & International Studies, pp. 61–70.

37. Zheng, Bojian; Wang, Liwen; and Chen, Shengho (1997). "The Development and Prospect of Hong Kong Funded Enterprises in Guangdong," *The Ninth Five Year Plan, the Long-term Target for the Year 2010, and the Hong Kong Economy*. Hong Kong: The Better Hong Kong Foundation, and One Country Two Systems Economic Research Institute. Vol. I, pp. 95–124.

Index

175

About the Author

Dr. Yun-Wing Sung obtained his Bachelor's Degree from the University of Hong Kong (1970) and his Ph.D. Degree in Economics from the University of Minnesota (1979). He is currently Professor and Chairman of Economics Department, and Co-Director of the Hong Kong and Asia-Pacific Economies Research Programme at the Chinese University of Hong Kong. He is the author / co-editor of *The China–Hong Kong Connection: The Key to China's Open-Door Policy* and *The Fifth Dragon: The Emergence of the Pearl River Delta*. He co-edited *The Other Hong Kong Report 1991, Studies on Economic Reform and Development in the People's Republic of China,* and *Shanghai: A City in Transformation*.

Dr. Sung specializes in trade and development of Mainland China, Hong Kong, and Taiwan. He has been visiting scholar at the Economics Department of the University of Chicago, the Harvard-Yenching Institute, and also the Economics Department of the University of Nottingham. He has served as consultant to the National Development Centre at the Australian National University, Asian Productivity Organisation, International Development Research Centre of Canada, the Hong Kong Tourist Association, and the Equal Opportunity Commission of Hong Kong.

The Hong Kong Economic Policy Studies Series

Titles	Authors
Hong Kong and the Region	
❏ The Political Economy of Laissez Faire	Yue-Chim Richard WONG
❏ Hong Kong and South China: The Economic Synergy	Yun-Wing SUNG
❏ Inflation in Hong Kong	Alan K. F. SIU
❏ Trade and Investment: Mainland China, Hong Kong and Taiwan	K. C. FUNG
❏ Tourism and the Hong Kong Economy	Kai-Sun KWONG
❏ Economic Relations between Hong Kong and the Pacific Community	Yiu-Kwan FAN
Money and Finance	
❏ The Monetary System of Hong Kong	Y. F. LUK
❏ The Linked Exchange Rate System	Yum-Keung KWAN Francis T. LUI
❏ Hong Kong as an International Financial Centre: Evolution, Prospects and Policies	Y. C. JAO
❏ Corporate Governance: Listed Companies in Hong Kong	Richard Yan-Ki HO Stephen Y. L. CHEUNG
❏ Institutional Development of the Insurance Industry	Ben T. YU
Infrastructure and Industry	
❏ Technology and Industry	Kai-Sun KWONG
❏ Competition Policy and the Regulation of Business	Leonard K. CHENG Changqi WU
❏ Telecom Policy and Digital Convergence	Milton MUELLER
❏ Port Facilities and Container Handling Services	Leonard K. CHENG Yue-Chim Richard WONG

Titles	Authors
❏ Efficient Transport Policy	Timothy D. HAU Stephen CHING
❏ Competition in Energy	Pun-Lee LAM
❏ Privatizing Water and Sewage Services	Pun-Lee LAM Yue-Cheong CHAN

Immigration and Human Resources

❏ Labour Market in a Dynamic Economy	Wing SUEN William CHAN
❏ Immigration and the Economy of Hong Kong	Kit Chun LAM Pak Wai LIU
❏ Youth, Society and the Economy	Rosanna WONG Paul CHAN

Housing and Land

❏ The Private Residential Market	Alan K. F. SIU
❏ On Privatizing Public Housing	Yue-Chim Richard WONG
❏ Housing Policy for the 21st Century: Homes for All	Rosanna WONG
❏ Financial and Property Markets: Interactions Between the Mainland and Hong Kong	Pui-King LAU
❏ Town Planning in Hong Kong: A Critical Review	Lawrence Wai-Chung LAI

Social Issues

❏ Retirement Protection: A Plan for Hong Kong	Francis T. LUI
❏ Income Inequality and Economic Development	Hon-Kwong LUI
❏ Health Care Delivery and Financing: A Model for Reform	Lok Sang HO
❏ Economics of Crime and Punishment	Siu Fai LEUNG